Reinventing *the* Classics

Edited by Dana Cowin

FOOD&**WINE**

FOOD & WINE REINVENTING THE CLASSICS

EDITOR **Kate Heddings**
DESIGN DIRECTOR **Patricia Sanchez, Nice Kern, LLC**
SENIOR EDITOR **Colleen McKinney**
ASSISTANT WINE EDITOR **Megan Krigbaum**
COPY EDITOR **Lisa Leventer**
DEPUTY PHOTO EDITOR **Anthony LaSala**
PRODUCTION MANAGER **Matt Carson**

FOOD & WINE

S.V.P./EDITOR IN CHIEF **Dana Cowin**
CREATIVE DIRECTOR **Stephen Scoble**
MANAGING EDITOR **Mary Ellen Ward**
EXECUTIVE EDITOR **Pamela Kaufman**
EXECUTIVE FOOD EDITOR **Tina Ujlaki**
ART DIRECTOR **Courtney Waddell Eckersley**
EXECUTIVE WINE EDITOR **Ray Isle**
EXECUTIVE ONLINE EDITOR **Rebecca Bauer**

AMERICAN EXPRESS PUBLISHING CORPORATION

PRESIDENT/C.E.O. **Ed Kelly**
CHIEF MARKETING OFFICER & PRESIDENT, DIGITAL MEDIA
   Mark V. Stanich
S.V.P./CHIEF FINANCIAL OFFICER **Paul B. Francis**
V.P./GENERAL MANAGERS **Frank Bland, Keith Strohmeier**

V.P., BOOKS & PRODUCTS/PUBLISHER **Marshall Corey**
DIRECTOR, BOOK PROGRAMS **Bruce Spanier**
SENIOR MARKETING MANAGER, BRANDED BOOKS **Eric Lucie**
ASSISTANT MARKETING MANAGER **Lizabeth Clark**
DIRECTOR OF FULFILLMENT & PREMIUM VALUE **Phil Black**
MANAGER OF CUSTOMER EXPERIENCE & PRODUCT DEVELOPMENT
   Charles Graver
DIRECTOR OF FINANCE **Thomas Noonan**
ASSOCIATE BUSINESS MANAGER **Uma Mahabir**
OPERATIONS DIRECTOR (PREPRESS) **Rosalie Abatemarco Samat**
OPERATIONS DIRECTOR (MANUFACTURING) **Anthony White**

FRONT COVER

PHOTOGRAPHER **Anna Williams**
FOOD STYLIST **Alison Attenborough**
STYLE EDITOR **Jessica Romm**

BACK COVER PHOTOGRAPHS

CHICKEN DRUMSTICKS **Con Poulos**
SHRIMP SCAMPI **Con Poulos**
BERRY SPOON CAKE **Lucy Schaeffer**
STICKY BUN **Con Poulos**
BROCCOLINI **Anson Smart**
TOMATO SOUP **James Baigrie**
GRILLED LAMB CHOPS **Con Poulos**
STUFFED SQUASH **John Kernick**

FLAP PHOTOGRAPH

PORTRAIT PHOTOGRAPHER **Andrew French**

TIME HOME ENTERTAINMENT

PUBLISHER **Richard Fraiman**
GENERAL MANAGER **Steven Sandonato**
EXECUTIVE DIRECTOR, MARKETING SERVICES **Carol Pittard**
DIRECTOR, RETAIL & SPECIAL SALES **Tom Mifsud**
DIRECTOR, NEW PRODUCT DEVELOPMENT **Peter Harper**
DIRECTOR, BOOKAZINE DEVELOPMENT & MARKETING
   Laura Adam
PUBLISHING DIRECTOR, BRAND MARKETING **Joy Butts**
ASSISTANT GENERAL COUNSEL **Helen Wan**
DESIGN & PREPRESS MANAGER **Anne-Michelle Gallero**
BOOK PRODUCTION MANAGER **Susan Chodakiewicz**
ASSOCIATE MANAGER, PRODUCT MARKETING **Nina Fleishman**

Reinventing
the Classics

Simple & creative ways to rethink the recipes
America loves best, with wines to match

FOOD&WINE
BOOKS

American Express Publishing Corporation, New York

Lemon Meringue
Cupcakes, p. 236

What's the one quality that makes a FOOD & WINE recipe different from any other recipe? I'd have to say it's accessible creativity.

At the magazine, we specialize in giving delicious twists to the classics everybody loves and craves. And that's what this book is all about: exciting new ideas for the tried-and-true. Perfected by our Test Kitchen and paired with wines in our Tasting Room, the recipes here are ideal for the novice who wants to confidently impress as well as the accomplished cook looking to add to an already formidable repertoire. Whether you try the chicken potpie with a topping of buttery toast instead of a time-consuming crust, or the spaghetti with baseball-size meatballs, I hope we've reinvented your own personal favorites and created some new ones.

Dana Cowin

Dana Cowin
EDITOR IN CHIEF, FOOD & WINE

Starters & Soups

Tiki Snack Mix

Honey-glazed peanuts are a classic bar snack. For this Polynesian-inspired version, FOOD & WINE's Melissa Rubel Jacobson mixes the nuts with sweet-salty bacon and chewy glazed pineapple to get all kinds of pupu-platter flavors into every bite.

INGREDIENTS

8 thick slices of meaty bacon

3 cups salted roasted peanuts

4 candied pineapple rings, cut into ⅓-inch triangles

2 tablespoons sesame seeds

1 tablespoon low-sodium soy sauce

1 tablespoon honey

¼ teaspoon cayenne pepper

Kosher salt

MAKES 4½ CUPS | ACTIVE: 15 MIN; TOTAL: 1 HR 15 MIN

1 Preheat the oven to 350°. Arrange the bacon slices in a single layer on a rack set over a large rimmed baking sheet. Bake for about 30 minutes, until the bacon is crisp. Drain the bacon on paper towels and cut into ½-inch strips.

2 In a bowl, toss the bacon with the peanuts, pineapple, sesame seeds, soy sauce, honey and cayenne. Spread on a rimmed baking sheet and bake for 20 minutes, stirring once, until the bacon is browned. Season the mix with salt and stir occasionally until cool, then serve.

Goat Cheese & Edamame Dip *with* Spiced Pepitas

This clever, creamy dip from recipe developer Rachel Soszynski looks like guacamole; however, it gets its pale green color not from avocados but from protein-and-fiber-rich soybeans, a.k.a. edamame. Sour cream and goat cheese make it luxurious, while canned chipotles in adobo sauce add heat and smokiness. The spiced *pepitas* (roasted and salted pumpkin seeds) scattered on top of the dip are great as a snack on their own.

INGREDIENTS

DIP

- 1½ pounds shelled edamame
- 1 cup sour cream
- 5 ounces fresh goat cheese, crumbled
- 3 chipotles in adobo, chopped, plus 2 tablespoons of adobo sauce from the can
- ¼ cup fresh lemon juice
- 1 small garlic clove, chopped
- 2 teaspoons kosher salt
- 1 tablespoon chopped oregano

PEPITAS

- ½ cup raw pumpkin seeds
- 1 teaspoon extra-virgin olive oil
- ½ teaspoon salt
- ¼ teaspoon ground coriander
- ¼ teaspoon crushed red pepper
- 1 teaspoon finely grated lemon zest
- 1 teaspoon chopped oregano

MAKES 4 CUPS | TOTAL: 40 MIN PLUS 1 HR CHILLING

1 Make the dip In a medium pot of boiling salted water, simmer the edamame until tender, about 8 minutes. Drain well and transfer to a food processor. Add the sour cream, goat cheese, chipotles, adobo sauce, lemon juice, garlic and salt to the processor and puree until smooth, scraping down the side of the bowl. Stir in the oregano and transfer the dip to a serving bowl. Cover with plastic wrap and refrigerate for at least 1 hour or overnight.

2 Make the pepitas Preheat the oven to 375°. On a rimmed baking sheet, toss the pumpkin seeds with the olive oil, salt, coriander and crushed red pepper. Bake for about 7 minutes, until the pumpkin seeds begin to brown. Transfer the *pepitas* to a bowl and toss with the lemon zest and oregano.

3 Serve the dip at room temperature, topped with the *pepitas*.

MAKE AHEAD The dip can be refrigerated overnight; bring to room temperature before serving. The *pepitas* can be kept in an airtight container at room temperature for up to 3 days.

SERVE WITH Pita crisps.

Israeli Hummus *with* Whole Chickpeas

To make his classic-style hummus supersmooth, chef Michael Solomonov of Zahav in Philadelphia soaks dried chickpeas overnight with baking soda to soften them. Then he simmers the chickpeas with unpeeled garlic cloves (he peels them later) so that the chickpeas soak up the garlic flavor and the garlic becomes creamy and mellow. For garnish, Solomonov pulls out all the stops, topping the hummus with tahini, cumin, paprika, parsley, whole chickpeas and a generous drizzle of olive oil.

INGREDIENTS

½ pound dried chickpeas, soaked overnight in water with 1 tablespoon baking soda, then drained and rinsed

7 large garlic cloves, unpeeled

½ cup extra-virgin olive oil, plus more for drizzling

¼ teaspoon ground cumin, plus more for garnish

½ cup tahini, at room temperature (see Note)

¼ cup plus 1 tablespoon fresh lemon juice

Salt

Paprika, for garnish

¼ cup chopped flat-leaf parsley, for garnish

Pita chips, for serving

MAKES ABOUT 4 CUPS
ACTIVE: 15 MIN; TOTAL: 1 HR 15 MIN PLUS OVERNIGHT SOAKING

1 In a medium saucepan, cover the chickpeas and garlic with 2 inches of water; bring to a boil. Simmer over moderately low heat until the chickpeas are tender, about 40 minutes. Drain, reserving ⅔ cup of the cooking water and 2 tablespoons of the chickpeas. Rinse the chickpeas under cold water and peel the garlic cloves.

2 In a food processor, puree the chickpeas with ½ cup of the reserved cooking water, ¼ cup of the olive oil and 6 of the garlic cloves. Add the ¼ teaspoon of cumin and ¼ cup each of the tahini and lemon juice; process the mixture until creamy. Season the hummus with salt and transfer to a serving bowl.

3 Wipe out the food processor. Add the remaining tahini, olive oil, lemon juice, reserved cooking water and garlic clove and puree.

4 Using a ladle, make a well in the hummus, then spoon in the tahini mixture. Garnish the hummus with cumin, paprika, the reserved whole chickpeas and the chopped parsley. Drizzle with olive oil and serve with pita chips.

NOTE Tahini has a tendency to separate, so be sure to stir the sesame paste thoroughly before measuring.

MAKE AHEAD The ungarnished hummus and cooked chickpeas can be refrigerated separately for up to 2 days.

Guacamole *with* Charred Jalapeño & Scallions

FOOD & WINE's Grace Parisi grills garlic, scallions and a jalapeño pepper to give her guacamole a deep, smoky flavor. For a brighter, crunchier version, she finely chops the scallions, garlic and jalapeño and stirs them in raw.

INGREDIENTS

- 3 medium scallions, white and tender green parts only
- 2 medium garlic cloves, unpeeled
- 1 jalapeño, seeded and quartered lengthwise
- 1 tablespoon vegetable oil
- 3 Hass avocados, halved and pitted
- ¼ cup finely chopped cilantro
- 2 tablespoons fresh lime juice

Salt and freshly ground pepper

MAKES 2 CUPS | | **TOTAL: 20 MIN**

1 Preheat a grill pan. In a small bowl, toss the scallions, garlic and jalapeño pepper with the vegetable oil. Grill over moderately high heat, turning occasionally, until the vegetables are charred all over, 5 to 6 minutes. Transfer to a work surface and let cool.

2 Finely chop the scallions and jalapeño and transfer to a medium bowl. Peel the garlic cloves, mash them to a paste and add them to the bowl. Scoop the avocado flesh into the bowl and coarsely mash with a fork. Fold the cilantro and lime juice into the guacamole, season with salt and pepper and serve.

SERVE WITH Fried tortilla strips.

Grilled Tomato Crostini

Instead of roasting the tomatoes in the oven for this wonderful summer appetizer, FOOD & WINE's Melissa Rubel Jacobson grills them outside in foil packets— a smart way to take advantage of hot coals while keeping the kitchen cool. She toasts ciabatta slices on the grill, too, then spoons the soft, sweet tomatoes on the bread (making sure to include some of their delicious juices), drizzles the crostini with olive oil and scatters basil leaves on top.

INGREDIENTS

- 4 tomatoes (1 pound), quartered
- 1 pint grape or cherry tomatoes (10 ounces)
- 1 pint small mixed heirloom tomatoes, halved if large
- ½ cup extra-virgin olive oil, plus more for drizzling
- Kosher salt and freshly ground pepper
- Four ¾-inch-thick slices of ciabatta bread
- 1 garlic clove, halved
- 20 small basil leaves

4 SERVINGS | :) | TOTAL: 30 MIN

1 Light a grill. Arrange four 12-by-24-inch sheets of heavy-duty aluminum foil on a work surface. Mound the tomatoes in the center of each sheet, drizzle with the ½ cup of olive oil and season with salt and pepper. Fold up the foil to create tight packets. Poke small holes in the top of each packet.

2 Set the packets on the grill and cover. Grill over moderately high heat for about 18 minutes, until the tomatoes begin to soften and burst. Meanwhile, grill the ciabatta slices until toasted and charred in spots, about 1 minute per side. Transfer the bread to plates and rub with the garlic halves.

3 Using scissors, carefully cut open the foil packets. Spoon the tomatoes and their juices over the grilled bread and drizzle with olive oil. Sprinkle with salt and basil and serve.

Tomatoes have so much tanginess that they need a wine with equal acidity as a balance. Sparkling rosé is just the thing. Try the NV Gruet Brut Rosé from New Mexico or the 2007 Argyle Brut Rosé from Oregon.

Shrimp & Vegetable Summer Rolls

These healthy, pretty Vietnamese summer rolls from FOOD & WINE's Melissa Rubel Jacobson get crunch and color from lettuce, carrots and the unusual addition of red bell peppers. For extra flavor and visual contrast, Melissa suggests sprinkling toasted black sesame seeds inside or over the rolls.

Shrimp's sweetness makes it one of the rare ingredients that almost always go well with an off-dry (slightly sweet) white. Off-dry Riesling, in particular, pairs nicely with these rolls—the 2009 Charles Smith Wines Kung Fu Girl from Washington State, perhaps, or the 2008 Willamette Valley Vineyards Riesling from Oregon.

INGREDIENTS

- 2 cups shredded carrots
- 1 small red onion, thinly sliced
- ¾ cup plus 2 tablespoons unseasoned rice vinegar
- ½ cup sugar
- 2 garlic cloves, smashed
- 1 tablespoon Asian fish sauce
- Sixteen 8-inch round rice papers
- 16 cilantro sprigs

- 1 head of Boston lettuce, separated
- 1 pound cooked large shrimp, halved lengthwise
- 2 red or yellow bell peppers, cut into ¼-inch strips
- 3½ ounces bean thread vermicelli, soaked in hot water until pliable and drained well

8 SERVINGS | ACTIVE: 40 MIN; TOTAL: 1 HR 15 MIN

1 In a bowl, toss the carrots and onion with ¼ cup plus 2 tablespoons of the rice vinegar and 2 tablespoons of the sugar. Let stand until the vegetables soften, about 30 minutes. Drain the pickled vegetables.

2 Meanwhile, in a glass bowl, mix the remaining rice vinegar and sugar with the garlic, then microwave at high power for about 30 seconds, until the sugar is dissolved. Add the fish sauce and set aside for 30 minutes; discard the garlic.

3 Soak 1 rice paper at a time in hot water until pliable, about 10 seconds; transfer to a work surface. Set a cilantro sprig and lettuce leaf on the lower third of the rice paper and top with 3 shrimp halves. Top with some of the bell pepper, vermicelli and the pickled vegetables; roll up tightly, folding in the sides. Place the roll on a platter and repeat with the remaining ingredients. Halve the summer rolls and serve with the sauce for dipping.

Goat-Cheese-Stuffed Grape Leaves

Inspired by Turkey's rice-stuffed grape leaves (dolmas), star chef Mehmet Gürs of Istanbul's Mikla restaurant ingeniously wraps goat cheese in the briny leaves, then quickly grills the little packages to melt the cheese. An added surprise: He flavors the filling with an aromatic mix of thyme, rosemary and lavender.

INGREDIENTS

- 12 jarred grape leaves
- 1 teaspoon minced dried thyme
- 1 teaspoon minced dried rosemary
- 1 teaspoon minced dried lavender
- One 12-ounce log of soft goat cheese, chilled
- Salt
- 2 tablespoons extra-virgin olive oil, plus more for brushing
- Grilled bread, for serving (optional)

MAKES 12 PACKAGES | TOTAL: 1 HR

1 Bring a medium saucepan of water to a boil. Add the grape leaves and boil for 30 seconds; drain. Blanch the leaves a second time in fresh boiling water. Drain again, pat dry and cut off the stems. Spread the leaves out on a work surface, vein side up.

2 Light a grill or heat a grill pan. In a shallow dish, combine the thyme, rosemary and lavender. Cut the goat cheese into 12 equal rounds. Lightly roll the edge of each round in the herbs. Set a round in the center of each grape leaf and season lightly with salt. Drizzle each round with ½ teaspoon of olive oil and wrap them in the leaves. Lightly brush the packages with olive oil.

3 Grill the packages over moderately high heat for 2 minutes per side, until the leaves are crisp on the outside and the cheese is slightly melted. Serve with grilled bread.

Grilled Tofu *with* Asparagus & Nori Vinaigrette

Lee Anne Wong, supervising culinary producer for Bravo's *Top Chef,* pairs a European vegetable with Asian flavors, tossing asparagus in sesame oil, roasting it and serving it with grilled marinated tofu. Healthy recipes like this helped Wong lose more than 50 pounds.

Grown in the stony soil of France's Vouvray region, Chenin Blanc often tastes a bit smoky and a bit like green tea, which helps it pair beautifully with lighter grilled foods like this tofu. Consider the 2008 Jean-Claude & Christophe Pichot or search out the 2008 Domaine de la Taille aux Loups Les Caburoches.

INGREDIENTS

- ¼ cup rice vinegar
- 3 tablespoons white miso (fermented soybean paste)
- 2½ tablespoons soy sauce
- 1 tablespoon tahini paste
- 1 tablespoon agave nectar (see Note)
- 2 teaspoons mirin
- ⅛ teaspoon Chinese five-spice powder
- 1 pound extra-firm tofu, drained and cut into 4 blocks
- ¼ cup vegetable oil, plus more for the grill
- Three 7-by-8-inch sheets of toasted nori (seaweed), cut into strips

- ½ cup water
- 1 tablespoon honey
- 1 tablespoon fresh lemon juice
- ¼ teaspoon *sambal oelek* or other Asian chile paste
- Salt and freshly ground black pepper
- 1 pound medium asparagus
- 1 teaspoon toasted sesame oil
- ¼ teaspoon crushed red pepper
- 2 teaspoons sesame seeds
- ½ cup cilantro leaves
- 1 large scallion, thinly sliced

4 SERVINGS | **TOTAL: 50 MIN**

1. Preheat the oven to 425°. In a medium baking dish, whisk 2 tablespoons of the rice vinegar, 2 tablespoons of the miso and 1½ tablespoons of the soy sauce with the tahini paste, agave nectar, mirin and Chinese five-spice powder until smooth. Add the tofu and turn to coat. Let stand for 30 minutes.

2. Meanwhile, in a blender, combine the ¼ cup of vegetable oil with the nori, water, honey, lemon juice, *sambal oelek* and the remaining 2 tablespoons of rice vinegar, 1 tablespoon of miso paste and 1 tablespoon of soy sauce. Puree until smooth and season lightly with salt and black pepper. Refrigerate the nori vinaigrette.

3. On a baking sheet, toss the asparagus with the sesame oil; season with salt, black pepper and the crushed red pepper. Roast for about 10 minutes, until tender and browned.

4. Meanwhile, in a skillet, toast the sesame seeds over moderate heat until fragrant and lightly browned, about 1 minute. Let cool.

5. Light a grill and brush with vegetable oil. Remove the tofu from the marinade and grill over moderate heat, turning once, until browned and heated through, 6 minutes. Cut each block into 3 slices.

6. Spoon some of the nori vinaigrette onto plates. Top with the asparagus and tofu. Sprinkle with the toasted sesame seeds, cilantro and scallion and serve.

NOTE Sweet agave nectar, made from the agave plant, is available at health-food stores and Whole Foods Market.

Tomato Tartlets

FOOD & WINE's Grace Parisi deconstructed the traditional French tomato tart and came up with this amazingly fast and easy hors d'oeuvre. Her stroke of genius: Instead of making individual tarts, she prebakes a large rectangle of puff pastry, spreads on silky pureed ricotta cheese, tops it with oven-roasted cherry tomatoes, cuts and serves.

 Lambrusco, Emilia-Romagna's delicious sparkling red, is great with starters like these tartlets because its effervescence refreshes the palate. Try the 2009 Medici Ermete Solo Reggiano or the NV Cantine Ceci La Luna.

INGREDIENTS

All-purpose flour, for rolling
½ pound all-butter puff pastry
30 cherry tomatoes (about 1 pound), halved crosswise
2 tablespoons extra-virgin olive oil

2 teaspoons thyme leaves, plus more for garnish
Kosher salt and freshly ground pepper
½ pound fresh ricotta cheese

MAKES 5 DOZEN PIECES | ⏱ | TOTAL: 45 MIN

1 Preheat the oven to 425° and line a large baking sheet with parchment paper. Position racks in the middle and upper thirds of the oven. On a lightly floured surface, roll out the puff pastry to a 9½-by-17½-inch rectangle. Using a straight edge, trim the pastry to a 9-by-17-inch rectangle. Transfer the pastry to the baking sheet and poke all over with a fork. Top with another sheet of parchment and another baking sheet and bake for 25 minutes on the middle rack, until golden. Remove the top baking sheet and parchment paper and bake the pastry until lightly browned and dry, about 10 minutes longer. Slide the paper and pastry onto a rack and let cool.

2 Meanwhile, in a large bowl, toss the tomatoes with the olive oil and 2 teaspoons of thyme and season with salt and pepper. Place the tomatoes on a baking sheet, cut side up, and bake on the upper rack for about 15 minutes, until softened slightly. Let cool.

3 In a food processor, puree the ricotta cheese until very creamy. Spread the ricotta over the cooled pastry and season with salt and pepper. Arrange the tomatoes cut side up on the ricotta in 5 rows of 12. Sprinkle lightly with thyme leaves. Using a long knife, cut the pastry between the tomatoes into 60 squares. Transfer the tartlets to platters and serve them at once.

MAKE AHEAD The recipe can be prepared through Step 2 and kept at room temperature for up to 8 hours.

Smoky Tomato Soup *with* Gruyère Toasts

In this inventive take on the classic combination of grilled cheese and tomato soup, FOOD & WINE's Melissa Rubel Jacobson uses the sweetest, ripest tomatoes in season to make a soup she flavors with mild Spanish smoked paprika (pimentón). She serves nutty Gruyère cheese toasts alongside.

When pairing tomatoes with wine, it's important to choose a variety that has similar bright acidity. Try an unoaked Chardonnay like the 2009 Lioco Sonoma County or the 2009 Healdsburg Ranches.

INGREDIENTS

- 1 tablespoon unsalted butter
- 1 tablespoon extra-virgin olive oil
- 1 onion, cut into ¼-inch dice
- 2 garlic cloves, crushed
- 2 teaspoons sweet smoked paprika, preferably pimentón de la Vera
- 3½ pounds tomatoes, quartered
- ½ cup water
- 1 thyme sprig
- 1 bay leaf
- Kosher salt and freshly ground pepper
- ¼ cup plus 2 tablespoons heavy cream
- Eight ¼-inch-thick baguette slices, cut on the bias
- 2 ounces Gruyère cheese, coarsely grated (¾ cup)

4 SERVINGS | ☺ | TOTAL: 40 MIN

1 In a soup pot, melt the butter in the olive oil. Add the onion and garlic and cook over moderately high heat until tender, about 5 minutes. Add the paprika and cook until fragrant, about 30 seconds. Add the tomatoes, water, thyme sprig and bay leaf, season with salt and pepper and bring the tomato mixture to a boil. Cover and simmer over moderate heat until the tomatoes break down, about 15 minutes. Discard the thyme sprig and bay leaf.

2 Preheat the broiler. In a blender, carefully puree the soup in batches until smooth. Strain the soup back into the pot, pressing on the solids to extract as much soup as possible. Stir the cream into the soup and season with salt and pepper.

3 Meanwhile, place the baguette slices on a baking sheet. Broil 6 inches from the heat until lightly toasted on both sides, about 2 minutes total. Top the toasts with the Gruyère and broil for about 30 seconds, until the cheese is bubbly. Ladle the soup into bowls and serve with the Gruyère toasts.

MAKE AHEAD The soup can be refrigerated for up to 2 days.

Chilled Spring Pea Soup

Spring pea soup can be a very labor-intensive recipe, since it ordinarily calls for fresh English peas that must be shelled. But this adaptation of a signature recipe from star chef Daniel Boulud calls for sugar snaps and frozen baby peas, which don't require shelling.

Lively, grassy Austrian Grüner Veltliner is an unparalleled match for spring vegetables like the peas in this soup. Pour the 2009 Loimer Lois or the 2009 Grooner.

INGREDIENTS

- 8 slices of bacon
- 1 tablespoon extra-virgin olive oil
- 2 celery ribs, thinly sliced
- 1 onion, thinly sliced
- 1 leek, white and tender green parts only, thinly sliced
- 5 cups chicken stock or low-sodium broth
- Two 4-inch rosemary sprigs
- Salt and freshly ground white pepper
- ½ pound sugar snap peas, thinly sliced
- Two 10-ounce boxes frozen baby peas
- ¼ cup flat-leaf parsley leaves
- 1 cup heavy cream
- 1 garlic clove, minced

6 SERVINGS | ☼ | TOTAL: 45 MIN

1 In a medium soup pot, cook the bacon over moderate heat until browned and crisp, about 6 minutes. Transfer the bacon to a plate. Pour off the fat in the pot.

2 In the same pot, heat the olive oil. Add the celery, onion and leek and cook over moderately low heat, stirring occasionally, until softened but not browned, about 7 minutes. Add the chicken stock, 4 slices of the cooked bacon, 1 rosemary sprig and a pinch each of salt and white pepper. Simmer until the vegetables are very tender, about 15 minutes. Discard the bacon and rosemary. Using a slotted spoon, transfer the vegetables to a blender.

3 Meanwhile, bring a medium saucepan of salted water to a boil. Add the sugar snaps and cook for 3 minutes. Add the frozen baby peas and the parsley and cook just until heated through, about 1 minute; drain. Add the sugar snaps, baby peas and parsley to the blender and puree until smooth, adding a few tablespoons of the broth to loosen the mixture. Transfer the puree and the remaining broth to a large bowl set in a larger bowl of ice water and stir until cool.

4 In a small saucepan, bring the heavy cream, garlic and remaining rosemary sprig to a boil. Simmer over low heat until slightly reduced, about 5 minutes. Strain the garlic cream into a bowl and let cool.

5 Ladle the chilled pea soup into bowls and drizzle with the garlic cream. Crumble the remaining 4 slices of bacon into the bowls and serve the soup right away.

MAKE AHEAD The pea soup and garlic cream can be refrigerated separately for up to 2 days.

Black Bean Soup *with* Crispy Tortillas

This ultrasimple soup from FOOD & WINE's Melissa Rubel Jacobson requires little more than a couple of cans of black beans, some onion and a bit of cumin. The surprise ingredient is pickled jalapeño, which adds a nice bit of tanginess and heat.

Earthy black bean soup is delicious with a bold, lower-tannin red wine like Malbec. Look for the 2008 Catena from star producer Laura Catena or the 2006 Añoro from sommelier Ken Fredrickson.

INGREDIENTS

Vegetable oil, for frying

Three 6-inch corn tortillas, cut into narrow wedges

Kosher salt

1 onion, cut into ¼-inch dice

1 teaspoon ground cumin

1 pickled jalapeño, seeded and minced

Two 15-ounce cans black beans

2 tablespoons chopped cilantro

Freshly ground pepper

4 SERVINGS | :) | TOTAL: 35 MIN

1 In a medium saucepan, heat ½ inch of vegetable oil over moderately high heat until a deep-fry thermometer registers 350°. Add the tortillas and fry, stirring occasionally, until crisp and lightly golden, about 1½ minutes. Using a slotted spoon, transfer the tortillas to paper towels to drain; season with salt.

2 In a medium soup pot, heat 2 tablespoons of the oil used to fry the tortillas. Add the onion and cook over moderate heat until softened, about 6 minutes. Add the cumin and pickled jalapeño and cook for 1 minute. Add the beans and their liquid and 1½ cups of water. Bring to a simmer and cook until slightly thickened, about 15 minutes. Stir in 1 tablespoon of the cilantro and season with salt and pepper. Ladle the soup into bowls and top with a few tortillas. Sprinkle with the remaining 1 tablespoon of cilantro and serve.

MAKE AHEAD The soup can be refrigerated and the tortillas kept in an airtight container overnight.

Minestrone *with* Black-Eyed Peas & Kidney Beans

In this modern minestrone from L.A.'s Campanile, chef Mark Peel replaces cannellini beans with an earthy mix of kidney beans and black-eyed peas. And instead of adding the usual pasta (ditalini or another small pasta), he boils penne, slices it into rings and sautés them in olive oil so they're crispy-chewy.

INGREDIENTS

- 3 tablespoons extra-virgin olive oil
- 2 ounces pancetta, finely diced
- 1 large onion, finely chopped
- 2 celery ribs, thinly sliced
- 4 garlic cloves, thinly sliced
- 1 leek, white and tender green parts thinly sliced, 1 dark top reserved

Salt and freshly ground pepper

- ½ pound Savoy or other green cabbage, coarsely shredded

- One 14-ounce can diced tomatoes
- 1 cup dried black-eyed peas
- 2 quarts water
- 3 parsley sprigs
- 1 bay leaf
- 3 thyme sprigs
- One 15-ounce can red kidney beans, drained and rinsed
- 2 ounces penne
- ½ cup shredded basil
- ¼ cup plus 2 tablespoons grated Parmigiano-Reggiano cheese

6 SERVINGS | ACTIVE: 30 MIN; TOTAL: 1 HR 30 MIN

1 In a pot, heat 2 tablespoons of the oil. Add the pancetta, onion, celery, garlic and sliced leek and season with salt and pepper. Cook over moderate heat until the vegetables are softened, 10 minutes. Add the cabbage and cook until slightly wilted, 1 minute. Add the tomatoes and cook for about 5 minutes. Add the black-eyed peas and water; bring to a boil. Wrap the parsley, bay leaf and thyme in the reserved leek top and secure with kitchen twine. Add to the pot.

2 Cover the pot and simmer over low heat until the black-eyed peas are tender, 45 minutes. Discard the herbs. Add the kidney beans and simmer for 10 minutes longer.

3 Meanwhile, in a pot of boiling salted water, cook the penne until al dente. Drain and cool under running water. Slice the penne crosswise into ¼-inch rings.

4 In a nonstick skillet, heat the remaining 1 tablespoon of oil. Add the penne in a single layer and cook over moderately high heat, turning once, until golden, 5 minutes. Drain the penne rings on paper towels.

5 Stir the basil into the soup and ladle into bowls. Sprinkle each with some of the penne rings and 1 tablespoon of the cheese and serve.

MAKE AHEAD The soup can be refrigerated and the penne rings kept in an airtight container overnight.

Ginger-Beef Noodle Soup

Rather than using a soup pot set on the stove, FOOD & WINE's Grace Parisi uses a slow-cooker for her simple version of the Chinese beef noodle soup *niu rou mien*. Cooking the beef for several hours in a broth flavored with soy sauce, ginger, garlic and star anise infuses the meat with marvelous flavor and makes it unbelievably tender.

Burgundian Pinot Noir would be a great pairing for this mushroomy soup, because it offers earthy flavors, too. Consider the 2007 Domaine Pierre Morey Monthélie or the 2008 Chassagne-Montrachet Vieilles Vignes Rouge from Domaine Bernard Moreau et Fils.

INGREDIENTS

1½ pounds beef chuck in one piece

8 cups beef broth

4 cups water

½ cup soy sauce

½ cup plus 2 tablespoons very thinly sliced peeled fresh ginger (4 ounces)

1 onion, coarsely chopped

3 garlic cloves, thinly sliced

½ star anise pod

½ pound shiitake mushrooms, stems discarded and caps thickly sliced

3 large scallions, thinly sliced

1 pound fresh Chinese egg noodles or thick Japanese udon

Toasted sesame oil or hot chile oil, for serving

6 SERVINGS | ACTIVE: 20 MIN; TOTAL: 4 HR 45 MIN

1 In a slow cooker, combine the meat with the broth, water, soy sauce, ginger, onion, garlic and star anise. Cover and cook on high for 4 hours, until the meat is tender. Transfer the meat to a plate and let cool slightly. Using 2 forks, pull the meat into thick shreds.

2 Strain the broth, discarding the solids. Return the broth to the cooker. Add the shiitake, scallions and shredded meat. Cook on high for 15 minutes, until the mushrooms are tender.

3 Meanwhile, bring a large saucepan of salted water to a boil. Add the noodles and cook until al dente. Drain well.

4 Add the noodles to the soup. Serve in deep bowls, passing the sesame or chile oil at the table.

MAKE AHEAD The soup can be prepared through Step 2 and refrigerated for up to 4 days.

Pasta & Grains

Spaghetti *with* Bolognese Sauce

Classic Bolognese sauce (from northern Italy's Bologna region) is made with a mix of fresh and cured meats. In this version, FOOD & WINE's Marcia Kiesel uses a combination of meats—ground beef and pork, plus pancetta and pistachio-flecked mortadella—but increases the amounts to make the sauce extra hearty.

Rich, meaty Bolognese is great paired with powerful Barolo, because the heartiness of the dish balances the tannins in the wine. Good Barolos like the 2004 Ceretto Bricco Rocche Prapò and the 2004 Elvio Cogno Ravera Barolo are no bargain, but they're definitely worth the splurge.

INGREDIENTS

1 tablespoon unsalted butter
1 tablespoon extra-virgin olive oil
4 garlic cloves, minced
3 ounces thinly sliced pancetta, finely chopped
1 medium carrot, finely diced
1 medium onion, finely diced
1 celery rib, finely diced
1 pound coarsely ground beef chuck
1 pound coarsely ground pork
¼ pound mortadella, cut into ¼-inch dice (optional)
1 tablespoon tomato paste
1 cup dry white wine
One 28-ounce can Italian whole tomatoes, chopped, juices reserved
1½ cups chicken or beef stock or low-sodium broth
¼ teaspoon freshly grated nutmeg
3 tablespoons chopped flat-leaf parsley
2 tablespoons chopped basil
Salt and freshly ground pepper
1 pound spaghetti
¼ cup heavy cream
Freshly grated Parmesan cheese, for serving

6 SERVINGS | ACTIVE: 45 MIN; TOTAL: 2 HR 15 MIN

1 In a medium enameled cast-iron casserole, melt the butter in the oil. Add the garlic, pancetta, carrot, onion and celery and cook over moderately low heat until the onion is golden, about 5 minutes. Add the ground beef and pork and cook over moderate heat, breaking up the meat with a wooden spoon, until no pink remains, about 8 minutes. Stir in the mortadella and tomato paste and cook for 2 minutes. Add the wine and cook, stirring, until reduced by half, about 3 minutes. Add the tomatoes with their juices, the stock, nutmeg and 1 tablespoon each of the parsley and basil and bring to a boil. Season with salt and pepper and simmer over low heat, stirring occasionally, until very thick, about 1½ hours. Keep the sauce warm.

2 In a large pot of boiling salted water, cook the spaghetti until al dente. Drain and return the spaghetti to the pot.

3 Stir the cream and the remaining 2 tablespoons of parsley and 1 tablespoon of basil into the meat sauce. Season the sauce with salt and pepper, then add 2 cups to the spaghetti and toss. Transfer the spaghetti to a large bowl, top with the remaining sauce and serve. Pass the Parmesan cheese at the table.

MAKE AHEAD The Bolognese sauce can be refrigerated for up to 5 days.

Linguine *with* Walnut & Broccoli Rabe Pesto

FOOD & WINE's Melissa Rubel Jacobson opts for broccoli rabe instead of basil to give a pleasing bitterness to this earthy pesto. And in place of trenette (the classic noodle for pesto), she calls for the slightly thicker, easier-to-find linguine.

This recipe can easily be paired with a bright white wine or a medium-bodied red. Greg Brewer and Steve Clifton, winemakers at Santa Barbara County's Brewer-Clifton, have released two wines that would go equally well with this dish: the 2008 Santa Rita Hills Chardonnay and the 2008 Santa Rita Hills Pinot Noir.

INGREDIENTS

- ⅓ cup plus 2 tablespoons walnuts
- ½ pound broccoli rabe, trimmed
- 1 garlic clove
- ⅓ cup plus 1 tablespoon extra-virgin olive oil
- Pinch of crushed red pepper
- ⅓ cup freshly grated pecorino cheese, plus more for serving
- Kosher salt and freshly ground pepper
- ¾ pound linguine

4 SERVINGS | **TOTAL: 30 MIN**

1. Preheat the oven to 350°. Spread the walnuts in a pie plate and toast for 8 minutes, until fragrant and lightly golden; let cool. Chop 2 tablespoons of the walnuts.

2. In a large pot of boiling salted water, cook the broccoli rabe until tender, about 3 minutes. Drain and let cool under cold water. Squeeze out the excess water and coarsely chop the broccoli rabe.

3. In a food processor, mince the garlic. Add the ⅓ cup of walnuts; pulse until coarsely chopped. Add the broccoli rabe, olive oil and crushed red pepper and process until the broccoli rabe is very finely chopped. Add the ⅓ cup of pecorino and pulse until just combined. Season with salt and pepper. Scrape the pesto into a large bowl.

4. In a large pot of boiling salted water, cook the linguine until al dente. Drain, reserving ¾ cup of the pasta cooking water. Add the linguine to the pesto, then stir in the reserved cooking water and toss until the pasta is well coated with the pesto. Sprinkle with the chopped walnuts and serve at once, passing more pecorino at the table.

MAKE AHEAD The broccoli rabe pesto can be refrigerated overnight. Bring to room temperature before serving.

Bucatini Carbonara

Italian carbonara sauce is famously rich, combining pancetta or *guanciale* (cured pork jowl), egg yolks and cheese. This version from chef Linton Hopkins of Holeman and Finch Public House in Atlanta is even more luxurious: The sauce is enriched with heavy cream, and Hopkins uses thicker bucatini noodles (instead of spaghetti) to make the dish heartier.

INGREDIENTS

6 ounces bucatini or perciatelli

1 tablespoon extra-virgin olive oil

4 ounces pancetta, sliced ¼ inch thick and cut into ¼-inch dice

1 shallot, very finely chopped

1 garlic clove, very finely chopped

1 cup heavy cream

2 tablespoons freshly grated Parmigiano-Reggiano cheese, plus more for serving

4 large egg yolks

Salt

2 tablespoons chopped parsley

Freshly ground pepper

---

4 FIRST-COURSE SERVINGS | :) | TOTAL: 30 MIN

1 In a large pot of boiling salted water, cook the pasta until al dente. Drain, reserving 3 tablespoons of the cooking water.

2 Meanwhile, in a large skillet, heat the oil. Add the pancetta and cook over moderate heat until most of the fat has been rendered, 7 minutes. Add the shallot and garlic and cook over moderate heat for 1 minute. Add the cream and simmer over moderate heat until slightly thickened, about 2 minutes. Add the hot pasta to the skillet and stir to coat, 1 minute. Remove the skillet from the heat. Stir in the reserved pasta cooking water, the 2 tablespoons of grated cheese and the egg yolks. Season with salt. Divide the pasta into bowls and sprinkle with parsley and pepper. Serve, passing more cheese at the table.

An extravagant dish like carbonara pairs best with a tannic red that refreshes the palate. Look for a robust Vino Nobile di Montepulciano, from Tuscany, perhaps the 2005 Boscarelli or the 2005 Avignonesi.

Macaroni & Many Cheeses

Helen Jane Hearn and Natalie Wassum are founders of a California-based cheese-tasting club called Cheesewhizzes. At the end of their events, they gather any leftovers to make a fancy mac and cheese later in the week. The recipe, based on one from Marion Cunningham's *The Supper Book,* uses a mix of cheeses (none of which is cheddar). It works beautifully with any semihard cheese but is particularly good with an international blend of French Mimolette, aged Dutch Gouda and American Vella dry Jack.

INGREDIENTS

- 2 cups elbow macaroni
- 4 tablespoons unsalted butter
- ¼ cup all-purpose flour
- 3 cups milk
- 2 cups mixed shredded semihard cheeses, such as Mimolette, aged Gouda and Vella dry Jack (½ pound)
- Salt and freshly ground pepper
- ⅔ cup freshly grated Parmigiano-Reggiano cheese

4 TO 6 SERVINGS | :⊃ | TOTAL: 35 MIN

1 Preheat the broiler. In a medium saucepan of boiling salted water, cook the macaroni until al dente; drain well.

2 Meanwhile, in another medium saucepan, melt the butter over low heat. Whisk in the flour until a paste forms. Gradually whisk in the milk until smooth. Bring the sauce to a boil over moderately high heat, whisking, until thickened. Off the heat, stir in the mixed shredded cheeses until melted. Season with salt and pepper.

3 Add the macaroni to the hot cheese sauce and stir to coat; transfer to a 13-by-9-inch glass or ceramic baking dish and sprinkle on the Parmigiano-Reggiano. Broil 4 inches from the heat for 4 minutes, until richly browned. Let rest for 5 minutes before serving.

MAKE AHEAD The cheese sauce can be refrigerated for up to 2 days. Reheat thoroughly before adding the macaroni.

Grenache can be ripe and juicy enough to stand up to rich cheese dishes. Outpost's 2007 Howell Mountain from Napa or the 2008 Vinos de Terruños Siete 7 from Spain's Navarra region would be fabulous.

Flatbread Lasagna

For this supereasy lasagna spin-off, FOOD & WINE's Grace Parisi skips pasta sheets and layers pocketless pita bread or naan from the grocery with store-bought marinara sauce, hot Italian sausage and ricotta and mozzarella cheeses.

INGREDIENTS

- 1 pound hot Italian sausages, casings removed
- 1 tablespoon extra-virgin olive oil
- 1½ cups ricotta cheese

- Salt and freshly ground pepper
- 3 cups jarred marinara sauce
- 4 pocketless pita or naan
- 2 cups shredded mozzarella (12 ounces)

6 TO 8 SERVINGS | ACTIVE: 20 MIN; TOTAL: 1 HR 40 MIN

1 Preheat the oven to 350°. In a skillet, cook the sausages in the oil over moderately high heat, breaking up the meat, until browned. Season the ricotta with salt and pepper. Spread ½ cup of the marinara sauce in a deep-dish pie plate. Top with 1 flatbread, one-third of the sausage and ½ cup each of the ricotta and mozzarella. Repeat the layering twice more. Add ½ cup of sauce and the last flatbread. Top with the remaining 1 cup of sauce and ½ cup of mozzarella.

2 Cover the lasagna with foil and bake for 30 minutes. Uncover and bake 30 minutes longer. Let cool for 20 minutes and serve.

This decidedly inventive take on Italian lasagna happens to go well with an American Sangiovese full of vibrant red-berry fruit. Consider the 2006 Ca' del Solo from Bonny Doon Vineyard or the 2005 Ferrari-Carano Alexander Valley.

Parmigiano-Crusted Rigatoni *with* Cauliflower

Inspired by the classic Italian combination of cauliflower and prosciutto tossed with pasta and cream sauce, FOOD & WINE's Melissa Rubel Jacobson incorporates the ingredients into a baked casserole. For a quick, crunchy topping, she sprinkles the dish with a mixture of *panko* (Japanese bread crumbs) and Parmigiano and broils it. The topping browns perfectly in only 2 minutes.

Superrich pastas call for a full-bodied, brightly acidic white, like Italy's Verdicchio. Two good ones are the 2008 Bucci Classico and the 2008 Sartarelli Classico.

INGREDIENTS

- 3½ tablespoons extra-virgin olive oil
- 1 large garlic clove, thinly sliced
- 1 cup heavy cream
- Kosher salt and freshly ground pepper
- ¾ pound rigatoni

- One 1¾-pound head of cauliflower, cut into 1-inch florets
- 1 cup *panko* (Japanese bread crumbs)
- ½ cup freshly grated Parmigiano-Reggiano cheese
- 3 ounces sliced prosciutto, cut into ¼-inch-wide ribbons

4 SERVINGS | :) | **TOTAL: 30 MIN**

1 Preheat the broiler. Bring a large pot of salted water to a boil. In a medium skillet, heat 1 tablespoon of the olive oil. Add the garlic and cook over moderate heat until lightly golden, about 3 minutes. Add the cream and simmer until thickened slightly, about 2 minutes. Season the garlic cream with salt and pepper.

2 Cook the rigatoni until al dente; about 6 minutes before the rigatoni is done, add the cauliflower florets to the pot. Drain, reserving 2 tablespoons of the pasta cooking water.

3 Meanwhile, in a medium bowl, toss the *panko* with the Parmigiano and the remaining 2½ tablespoons of olive oil; season with salt and pepper.

4 Return the rigatoni and cauliflower to the pot. Add the garlic cream, the prosciutto and the reserved pasta water and toss until the pasta is coated. Scrape the pasta into a large, shallow baking dish and sprinkle the *panko* mixture evenly over the top. Broil for about 2 minutes, rotating constantly, until the topping is evenly browned. Serve hot.

Shiitake & Scallion Lo Mein

Lo mein is a Chinese dish of silky noodles tossed with stir-fried vegetables and often pork or chicken. Instead of using plates or bowls to serve her vegetarian lo mein, FOOD & WINE's Melissa Rubel Jacobson takes inspiration from Asian street-food carts and wraps the noodles in banana leaves.

Dolcetto d'Alba, from Piedmont, is not as well known as the region's Barolos and Barbarescos, but the light-bodied, fruit-forward red is a great partner for this earthy dish. Try the 2009 Pira or the 2008 Vietti Tre Vigne.

INGREDIENTS

- 1 pound wide lo mein noodles
- ¼ pound snow peas, halved diagonally
- ¼ cup soy sauce
- ¼ cup mirin
- 2 teaspoons toasted sesame oil
- 3 tablespoons canola oil
- 1 pound shiitake mushrooms, stems discarded and caps thinly sliced
- 6 scallions, cut into 1-inch lengths
- 1 tablespoon minced fresh ginger
- 2 tablespoons water
- 2 tablespoons chopped cilantro

Banana leaves, for serving (optional)

8 FIRST-COURSE SERVINGS | ⏱ | TOTAL: 40 MIN

1 In a large pot of boiling salted water, cook the noodles until tender; add the snow peas to the noodles in the last 2 minutes of cooking. Drain the noodles and snow peas and rinse under cold water until cool. In a small bowl, mix the soy sauce with the mirin and sesame oil.

2 In a very large, deep skillet, heat 2 tablespoons of the canola oil until shimmering. Add the shiitake mushrooms and cook over moderately high heat, undisturbed, until browned, about 5 minutes. Add the remaining 1 tablespoon of canola oil, the scallions and ginger and stir-fry until the scallions soften, about 3 minutes. Add the water and cook over moderate heat, scraping up the browned bits from the bottom of the pan, 1 minute. Add the noodles, snow peas and soy sauce mixture to the skillet and cook, tossing the noodles, until heated through, about 2 minutes. Add the cilantro, transfer to banana leaf cones or bowls and serve.

NOTE Banana leaves are available at Asian markets.

Red Curry Peanut Noodles

FOOD & WINE's Melissa Rubel Jacobson updates sesame noodles, a Chinese take-out staple, by swapping in pleasantly chewy whole-wheat spaghetti for the usual egg noodles and adding a hit of fiery red curry paste to the peanut sauce.

INGREDIENTS

¾ pound whole-wheat spaghetti

½ cup smooth peanut butter

1½ tablespoons fresh lime juice

1 tablespoon red curry paste

⅓ cup chicken stock
   or low-sodium broth

¼ cup plus 2 tablespoons
   packed cilantro leaves

Kosher salt

1 cup mung bean sprouts
   (2½ ounces)

2 scallions, quartered and thinly
   sliced lengthwise

1 carrot, coarsely grated

⅓ cup salted roasted peanuts,
   coarsely chopped

Lime wedges, for serving

4 SERVINGS | ⏲ | TOTAL: 25 MIN

1 In a large pot of boiling salted water, cook the spaghetti until al dente. Drain the spaghetti and rinse under cold water until cool. Drain very well.

2 Meanwhile, in a food processor, combine the peanut butter with the lime juice, red curry paste, stock and ¼ cup of the cilantro leaves and puree. Season the peanut sauce with salt.

3 In a large bowl, toss the spaghetti with the peanut sauce, bean sprouts, scallions and carrot until well coated. Season with salt. Transfer to bowls and sprinkle with the remaining cilantro leaves and the peanuts. Serve with lime wedges.

Dishes flavored with peanut butter always go well with malty beers because they share similar sweet, nutty notes. Look for a Summer Solstice Cerveza Crema from Anderson Valley Brewing Company or an Abita Turbodog, made in Abita Springs, Louisiana.

Rice-Noodle Salad *with* Chicken *&* Herbs

The usual citrusy dressing for this cool Vietnamese-style noodle salad is made with pomelo juice, but FOOD *&* WINE's Marcia Kiesel uses easy-to-find grapefruit juice instead.

Portugal's crisp, zippy Vinho Verde is great with dishes like this chicken salad. Try the 2009 Quinta de Gomariz or the 2009 Broadbent.

INGREDIENTS

½ pound dried rice noodles, about ¼ inch wide

¾ cup fresh grapefruit juice

2 large garlic cloves, minced

2 tablespoons sugar

¼ cup plus 1 tablespoon Asian fish sauce

½ pound cabbage, finely shredded (4 cups)

3 large scallions, thinly sliced

½ pound cooked chicken, cut into long strips

½ cup chopped cilantro

¼ cup chopped mint

¼ cup chopped roasted salted peanuts

Sriracha chile sauce, for serving

4 TO 6 SERVINGS | ACTIVE: 30 MIN; TOTAL: 1 HR

1 In a bowl, cover the noodles with cold water and let stand until pliable, 25 minutes. Drain. Bring a saucepan of water to a boil. Add the noodles and cook, stirring, until al dente, 1 minute. Drain the noodles in a colander and return them to the pan. Fill the saucepan with cold water and swish the noodles around. Drain and swish the noodles two more times. Drain the noodles in the colander, lifting and tossing, until dry.

2 In a small bowl, stir the grapefruit juice with the garlic, sugar and fish sauce until the sugar is dissolved.

3 In a large bowl, toss the rice noodles with the shredded cabbage and sliced scallions. Add the dressing and toss well. Add the chicken, cilantro, mint and peanuts and toss. Serve right away, passing Sriracha sauce at the table.

MAKE AHEAD The dressing can be refrigerated overnight.

Shrimp Fried Rice *with* Coconut & Pickled Onions

Chris Yeo, chef-partner of the Atlanta restaurant Straits, created this exquisite fried rice, known in Southeast Asia as *nasi goring*. In addition to firm, sweet shrimp, he uses two surprise ingredients: quick-pickled onion and nutty shredded coconut.

The American oak barrels often used for aging Chardonnay can impart a slight coconut aroma—which explains why oak-aged Chardonnay pairs well with this coconutty shrimp dish. Two to look for: the 2007 Shannon Ridge and the 2008 Trinitas Carneros.

INGREDIENTS

3 cups long-grain rice (19 ounces)
5 cups water
½ cup finely shredded fresh or dried unsweetened coconut
1 small onion, cut into ½-inch dice
3 tablespoons rice vinegar
Salt
2 medium carrots, cut into ½-inch dice
½ cup plus 2 tablespoons vegetable oil

4 large eggs, beaten
2 large shallots, thinly sliced
1 pound medium shrimp, shelled and deveined
Freshly ground white pepper
4 cups coarsely chopped green cabbage (½ small head)
1 teaspoon crushed red pepper
One 10-ounce package frozen peas, thawed
¼ cup Asian fish sauce

10 SERVINGS | ACTIVE: 35 MIN; TOTAL: 1 HR 30 MIN

1 In a large saucepan, rinse the rice, then drain it. Return the rice to the saucepan, add the water and bring to a boil. Cover and cook over low heat until the water is absorbed, about 15 minutes. Stir in the coconut, cover and let stand off the heat for 10 minutes. Fluff the rice and spread it out on a large rimmed baking sheet. Let cool, then refrigerate, uncovered, until chilled, about 1 hour.

2 Meanwhile, in a small bowl, toss the onion with the vinegar and a large pinch of salt. Let stand for 10 minutes.

3 In a small saucepan of boiling water, cook the carrots until tender, about 6 minutes. Drain and set aside.

4 In a nonstick skillet, heat 1 tablespoon of the oil. Season the eggs with salt, add to the skillet and cook over moderate heat, stirring a few times, until just scrambled, 1 minute. Transfer to a large plate.

5 Wipe out the skillet and heat 3 tablespoons of the oil. Add the shallots and cook over moderately high heat, stirring frequently, until browned and crisp, 2 minutes. Using a slotted spoon, transfer the shallots to the plate with the eggs. Add the shrimp to the skillet and season with salt and white pepper. Cook over moderate heat, turning once, until just cooked through, 2 minutes. Transfer to the large plate.

6 Rub the cooked rice between your hands to separate the grains. In each of 2 large skillets, heat 3 tablespoons of vegetable oil. Add half of the cabbage and crushed red pepper to each skillet and stir-fry over moderately high heat until softened, about 3 minutes. Add half of the peas, carrots and pickled onion to each skillet and stir until hot.

7 Add half of the rice to each skillet along with the shrimp and eggs; toss over moderate heat until well mixed and heated through, about 2 minutes. Remove from the heat and stir half of the fish sauce into the rice in each skillet. Season with salt and pepper. Transfer the rice to a large bowl, garnish with the fried shallots and serve.

Beet Risotto

Beets give this unexpected risotto from FOOD & WINE's Grace Parisi stunning color and delicate sweetness. To avoid staining hands and countertops, Grace suggests wearing rubber gloves and shredding the beets directly into a stainless steel bowl.

For this shockingly pink risotto, sparkling rosé, with its own depth and richness, is perfect. California's top producers use Champagne methods to make their sparkling wines but charge less than Champagne producers. Try the NV Domaine Carneros Cuvée de la Pompadour Brut Rosé or the 2006 Schramsberg Brut Rosé.

INGREDIENTS

- 7 cups chicken stock or 3½ cups low-sodium broth mixed with 3½ cups of water
- 4 tablespoons unsalted butter
- ¼ cup extra-virgin olive oil
- 1 large sweet onion, finely chopped
- 2 large beets (12 ounces each), peeled and coarsely shredded, plus thinly sliced beets for garnish
- 3 cups arborio rice (1¼ pounds)
- 6 ounces young pecorino cheese, freshly grated (1½ cups)
- 2 teaspoons poppy seeds, plus more for garnish

8 SERVINGS | TOTAL: 1 HR

1 In a medium saucepan, bring the stock to a simmer; cover and keep warm. In a medium enameled cast-iron casserole, melt the butter in the oil. Add the onion and cook over moderately high heat, stirring, until softened, about 5 minutes. Add the shredded beets and cook, stirring, until the pan is dry, about 12 minutes. Spoon half of the beets into a small bowl, leaving the remaining beets in the casserole.

2 Add the rice to the casserole and cook, stirring, for 2 minutes. Add 1 cup of the warm stock to the rice and cook over moderate heat, stirring, until the stock is nearly absorbed. Continue adding the stock 1 cup at a time, stirring constantly, until the rice is al dente and a thick sauce forms, about 22 minutes. Stir in the reserved cooked beets, the pecorino cheese and the 2 teaspoons of poppy seeds. Cook, stirring, until heated through; add a few tablespoons of water if the risotto is too thick. Spoon the risotto into bowls, garnish with thinly sliced beets and poppy seeds and serve right away.

Lemony Rice-Parsley Salad

Arborio rice is the magic ingredient in this easy, tangy salad from cookbook author Viana La Place. While most rice salads call for long-grain rice, arborio's high starch content produces a creamy texture that's terrific with fresh parsley and lemon juice and zest. And arborio cooks faster (in only 15 minutes) than long-grain rice, too.

INGREDIENTS

- 1 cup arborio rice
- ¼ cup extra-virgin olive oil
- 1 tablespoon fresh lemon juice
- 1 cup tightly packed flat-leaf parsley leaves, coarsely chopped
- ½ small sweet Italian frying pepper, cut into ¼-inch dice
- ⅓ cup oil-cured pitted black olives, coarsely chopped
- 1 tablespoon capers, rinsed and drained
- 1½ teaspoons grated lemon zest
- Salt and freshly ground pepper
- Lemon wedges, for serving

4 SERVINGS | | TOTAL: 25 MIN

1 Bring a large saucepan of salted water to a boil. Add the rice and simmer over moderate heat until just tender, about 14 minutes. Drain the rice thoroughly.

2 In a large bowl, toss the rice with the olive oil and lemon juice. Stir in the parsley, sweet Italian frying pepper, olives, capers and lemon zest and season with salt and pepper. Serve the rice salad warm or at room temperature, with lemon wedges.

Barley & Grilled-Vegetable Salad

Grilled vegetables are a summer party standard. FOOD & WINE's Grace Parisi mixes them with cooked barley, then tosses the salad with a nutty-herby dressing. A clever trick: Instead of turning on the oven, Grace sometimes toasts the walnuts on the grill, wrapping them in foil before placing them in the coals or on the grate.

Soave, a medium-bodied white from Italy's Veneto region, has a unique nutty note that's rare in unaged wines. It's a perfect partner for this grain salad. Look for the 2008 Inama Vin Soave Classico or the 2008 Prà Soave Classico.

INGREDIENTS

- 1 cup pearled barley (7 ounces)
- 2 zucchini, sliced diagonally ⅓ inch thick
- ½ pound shiitake mushrooms, stemmed
- ½ pound thick asparagus, peeled
- 1 red onion, sliced ⅓ inch thick
- ½ cup extra-virgin olive oil, plus more for brushing
- Salt and freshly ground pepper

- 1 cup walnuts
- 1 small shallot, very finely chopped
- 1 teaspoon thyme leaves
- 2 tablespoons fresh lemon juice
- ½ teaspoon finely grated lemon zest
- ¼ cup snipped chives
- 2 ounces fresh pecorino cheese, shaved (1 cup)

6 SERVINGS | TOTAL: 1 HR

1 Light a grill. In a large saucepan of boiling salted water, cook the barley over moderate heat until slightly tender, about 30 minutes. Drain and quickly rinse the barley under running water to cool it slightly. Shake off the water and transfer the barley to a large bowl.

2 Preheat the oven to 350°. Brush the zucchini, mushrooms, asparagus and onion with olive oil and season with salt and pepper. Grill the vegetables over high heat, turning occasionally, until lightly charred in spots and tender, 15 to 18 minutes. Transfer the grilled vegetables to a baking sheet and let cool. Cut into bite-size pieces and add to the barley.

3 Meanwhile, spread the walnuts in a pie plate and toast in the oven for about 12 minutes, until fragrant. Let cool completely.

4 Transfer the toasted walnuts to a food processor. Add the shallot, thyme, 1 tablespoon of the lemon juice, the lemon zest and the ½ cup of olive oil and pulse until the nuts are coarsely chopped. Season the dressing with salt and pepper and add to the barley and vegetables along with the remaining 1 tablespoon of lemon juice and the chives. Garnish with the shaved pecorino and serve warm.

Summer Farro Salad

Farro is a nutty, pleasantly chewy grain from Italy that's often cooked like pasta. Rather than boiling his farro in plain salted water, Marco Canora, chef-owner of Hearth in New York City, simmers it in water with sautéed onion, carrot and celery. The aromatic vegetables add delicate flavor to the cooked grains.

This summer salad calls for a vibrant Sauvignon Blanc, which goes incredibly well with fresh vegetables. Try the 2009 Hanna or the 2008 Handley, both from California.

INGREDIENTS

- ⅓ cup plus 2 tablespoons extra-virgin olive oil
- 1 small yellow onion, quartered
- 1 small carrot, halved
- 1 celery rib, halved
- 1¾ cups farro (12 ounces)
- 5 cups water
- Kosher salt

- 3 tablespoons red wine vinegar
- Freshly ground pepper
- ½ small red onion, thinly sliced
- 1 small seedless cucumber, halved lengthwise and thinly sliced crosswise
- 1 pint grape tomatoes, halved
- ¼ cup chopped fresh basil

8 SERVINGS | TOTAL: 35 MIN

1 In a large saucepan, heat 2 tablespoons of the olive oil. Add the yellow onion, carrot and celery, cover and cook over moderately low heat until the vegetables are barely softened, about 5 minutes. Add the farro and stir to coat with oil. Add the water and bring to a boil. Cover and simmer over low heat until the farro is barely tender, about 10 minutes; season with salt. Cover and simmer until the farro is al dente, about 10 minutes longer. Drain the farro and discard the onion, carrot and celery. Let cool completely.

2 In a large bowl, whisk the remaining ⅓ cup of olive oil with the red wine vinegar and season with salt and pepper. Fold in the farro, red onion, cucumber, tomatoes and basil, season the salad with salt and pepper and serve.

Quinoa Salad *with* Sugar Snap Peas

For this updated grain salad, FOOD & WINE's Marcia Kiesel opts for nutty quinoa (a grainlike seed) over more conventional choices like rice or barley. Not only does quinoa cook more quickly than most grains—15 minutes versus 60 for brown rice—it has a pleasing, slightly crunchy texture. And it's ridiculously good for you.

Vegetable dishes like this salad are terrific with unoaked whites like Sauvignon Blanc. New Zealand has become a mecca for Sauvignon Blanc, and 2009 was an exceptionally good year for the grape. Try the 2009 Babich Marlborough or the 2009 Dog Point Vineyard.

INGREDIENTS

- ½ pound sugar snap peas
- 1½ cups quinoa
- ¼ cup plus 1 tablespoon extra-virgin olive oil
- 3 tablespoons white wine vinegar
- Salt and freshly ground pepper
- ½ cup salted roasted pumpkin seeds
- ½ cup minced chives

6 SERVINGS | ACTIVE: 15 MIN; TOTAL: 40 MIN

1 In a small saucepan of boiling salted water, simmer the peas until bright green and crisp-tender, about 1 minute. Drain and spread out on a large plate to cool, then pat dry. Cut the peas on the diagonal into 1-inch pieces.

2 In a small saucepan, combine the quinoa with 2 cups of water and bring to a boil. Cover and cook over low heat until all of the water has evaporated and the quinoa is tender, about 15 minutes. Uncover and fluff the quinoa, then transfer to a large bowl and let cool to room temperature.

3 In a bowl, combine the oil and vinegar and season with salt and pepper. Add the peas to the quinoa along with the pumpkin seeds, chives and dressing; stir. Season the salad with salt and pepper and serve at room temperature or lightly chilled.

SERVE WITH Chilled tomato soup and fried tortilla strips.

MAKE AHEAD The salad can be refrigerated for up to 6 hours.

Roasted Squash *with* Quinoa Salad

Most stuffed-squash recipes call for baking a mixed-grain filling inside acorn squash or zucchini halves. Here, chef Michael Symon of Cleveland's Lola creates a stellar vegetarian main course by tossing quinoa with arugula, apple, raisins and fresh herbs, then spooning the cool salad into halved baked Delicata squash "bowls."

Chenin Blanc from Anjou in France's Loire region often has notes of apples, roasted nuts and honey, making it perfect with this squash dish. Agnès and René Mosse produce first-rate Chenin Blancs using biodynamic techniques, a holistic, organic approach to winemaking. Try the 2008 Mosse Les Bonnes Blanches or the more basic 2008 Mosse Anjou Blanc.

INGREDIENTS

- 2 Delicata squash (about 1 pound each), halved lengthwise and seeded
- 2 tablespoons extra-virgin olive oil
- Salt and freshly ground pepper
- 1 cup quinoa
- 2 tablespoons golden raisins
- 1 tablespoon sherry vinegar
- 1 teaspoon honey
- 1 Granny Smith apple, finely diced
- 1 large shallot, minced
- 1 garlic clove, minced
- 2 tablespoons chopped mint
- 2 tablespoons chopped parsley
- 2 ounces arugula (2 cups)

4 SERVINGS | ACTIVE: 30 MIN; TOTAL: 1 HR

1 Preheat the oven to 350°. Brush the cut sides of the squash with 1 teaspoon of the olive oil and season the cavities with salt and pepper. Place the squash cut side down on a baking sheet and roast for about 45 minutes, until tender.

2 Meanwhile, in a saucepan, bring 2 cups of lightly salted water to a boil. Add the quinoa, cover and simmer for 10 minutes. Stir in the raisins and simmer, covered, until the water is absorbed, about 5 minutes. Transfer the quinoa to a large bowl and let cool.

3 In a small bowl, whisk the vinegar and honey with the remaining 1 tablespoon plus 2 teaspoons of olive oil and season with salt and pepper. Add the dressing to the quinoa along with the apple, shallot, garlic, mint and parsley and toss well. Add the arugula and toss gently.

4 Set the roasted squash halves on plates, generously fill with the quinoa salad and serve.

MAKE AHEAD The quinoa salad can be refrigerated overnight. Bring to room temperature and add the arugula just before serving.

Seafood

Tuna *with* Provençal Vegetables

Instead of slowly stewing the vegetables as you would in a Provençal ratatouille, chef Bruce Sherman of Chicago's North Pond sautés zucchini and other summer vegetables with garlic, onion and thyme in only 10 minutes. The accompanying tuna is quickly pan-seared in garlicky olive oil.

For a white wine with enough weight to go with this meaty fish dish, consider Viognier. Although Viognier is one of the Rhône Valley's signature white grapes, producers from Texas to South Africa are growing it. Try the 2008 Domaine de Triennes Sainte Fleur from Provence or the 2009 Massena the Surly Muse from Australia.

INGREDIENTS

- ½ cup extra-virgin olive oil
- 1 pound zucchini, halved lengthwise and thinly sliced
- 1 red bell pepper, cut into thin strips
- ½ small red onion, thinly sliced
- 4 thyme sprigs
- 4 garlic cloves—2 thinly sliced, 2 halved

- Salt and freshly ground pepper
- 1 tomato, coarsely chopped
- 1 small fennel bulb—halved, cored and sliced paper-thin— plus fennel fronds for garnish
- ¼ cup pitted kalamata olives, coarsely chopped
- 1 tablespoon drained capers
- Four 5-ounce tuna steaks (1 inch thick)

4 SERVINGS | TOTAL: 40 MIN

1 In a large, deep skillet, heat ¼ cup of the olive oil. Add the zucchini, bell pepper, onion, thyme and sliced garlic and season with salt and pepper. Cook over high heat, stirring occasionally, until the vegetables are crisp-tender, about 7 minutes. Add the tomato, fennel, olives and capers, season with salt and pepper and cook, stirring, until the vegetables are tender, 2 to 3 minutes longer. Discard the thyme.

2 In a medium skillet, heat the remaining ¼ cup of oil with the halved garlic cloves. Season the tuna with salt and pepper, add it to the skillet and cook over moderate heat for 3 minutes, turning once. Cover the skillet and cook the tuna over very low heat for 2 minutes longer; the tuna should still be slightly rare in the center.

3 Spoon the vegetables onto plates. Top with the tuna steaks and the browned garlic halves, garnish with fennel fronds and serve.

Crisp Salmon *with* Avocado Salad

In her modern take on the quintessential ladies' luncheon dish of poached salmon with green salad, FOOD & WINE's Melissa Rubel Jacobson sears the salmon to give it a crispy crust and makes a wonderfully citrusy salad dressing by whisking fresh lemon and orange juices with a little mayonnaise and olive oil.

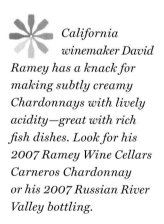 *California winemaker David Ramey has a knack for making subtly creamy Chardonnays with lively acidity—great with rich fish dishes. Look for his 2007 Ramey Wine Cellars Carneros Chardonnay or his 2007 Russian River Valley bottling.*

INGREDIENTS

- 2 tablespoons pine nuts
- 2½ tablespoons extra-virgin olive oil
- 2 tablespoons mayonnaise
- 1 tablespoon fresh lemon juice
- 1 tablespoon fresh orange juice
- Kosher salt and freshly ground black pepper
- Eight 6-ounce salmon fillets with skin
- 3 heads of Bibb lettuce, large leaves torn into bite-size pieces, small leaves left whole
- 2 Hass avocados, thinly sliced

8 SERVINGS | **TOTAL: 30 MIN**

1 In a small skillet, toast the pine nuts over moderate heat, tossing frequently, until golden, about 6 minutes. Transfer to a plate to cool. In a large bowl, whisk 1½ tablespoons of the olive oil with the mayonnaise, lemon juice and orange juice and season the dressing with salt and pepper.

2 Pat the salmon dry and season with salt and pepper. In a very large nonstick skillet, heat the remaining 1 tablespoon of olive oil over moderately high heat until shimmering. Add the salmon skin side down and cook until crisp and golden, about 6 minutes. Turn and cook the fillets until just pink in the center, about 4 minutes longer. Transfer the salmon to plates.

3 Add the Bibb lettuce, avocados and toasted pine nuts to the dressing and gently toss to coat. Mound the salad next to the salmon and serve.

Salmon *in* Tomato-Olive Sauce

At Philadelphia's El Rey, chef Dionicio Jimenez puts a Latin spin on Italy's puttanesca sauce (tomatoes, onions, capers, olives, oregano and garlic), spiking the recipe with pickled jalapeños to add an instant hit of tangy heat.

Dishes with olives are fun to pair with Pinot Noirs from New Zealand's Marlborough region because the wines often have savory flavors themselves. Match this salmon dish with the 2008 Grove Mill Pinot Noir or the 2008 Tohu Pinot Noir.

INGREDIENTS

- ¼ cup plus 1 tablespoon extra-virgin olive oil
- 1 medium onion, finely chopped
- 4 garlic cloves, finely chopped
- 2 pounds plum tomatoes, coarsely chopped
- 1 tablespoon chopped oregano
- 2 bay leaves
- ½ cup pitted kalamata olives, sliced
- ⅓ cup drained capers
- ⅓ cup sliced pickled jalapeños
- Four 7-ounce center-cut salmon fillets with skin
- Salt and freshly ground pepper

4 SERVINGS | TOTAL: 40 MIN

1 Preheat the oven to 375°. In a large saucepan, heat ¼ cup of the olive oil until shimmering. Add the onion and garlic and cook over moderately high heat, stirring occasionally, until softened, about 5 minutes. Add the tomatoes, oregano and bay leaves and cook, stirring occasionally, until the tomatoes are just beginning to break down, about 5 minutes. Stir in the olives, capers and jalapeños and simmer the sauce for 2 minutes longer. Discard the bay leaves.

2 In a large ovenproof skillet, heat the remaining 1 tablespoon of oil until shimmering. Season the salmon with salt and pepper and add to the skillet, skin side down. Cook over high heat until the skin begins to brown, about 4 minutes. Transfer the skillet to the oven and roast the fish for about 10 minutes, until slightly rare inside. Transfer the fish to plates, spoon the sauce all around and serve.

SERVE WITH Yellow rice and frisée salad.

Red Snapper *with* Citrus & Fennel Salad

Chefs have been serving fish with citrus salsas since the '80s. In this recipe, star chef Daniel Boulud replaces the salsa with a sweet, tangy and slightly spicy salad of grapefruit and orange sections, thinly sliced radishes and diced jalapeño. It's terrific with the broiled red snapper.

Tangy, minerally Albariño, from Spain's northwestern Rías Baixas region, is great with seafood. Try the 2008 Lagar de Costa or the 2008 Nora with this snapper and salad.

INGREDIENTS

- 4 small radishes, sliced paper-thin
- ½ small fennel bulb—halved, cored and shaved paper-thin
- ½ small red or yellow bell pepper, thinly sliced
- 1 jalapeño, seeded and finely diced
- ¼ cup coarsely chopped cilantro
- 1 tablespoon snipped chives
- 1 tablespoon finely shredded mint
- 1 grapefruit
- 1 navel orange
- 2 tablespoons extra-virgin olive oil, plus more for brushing
- 1 tablespoon fresh lemon juice

Salt and freshly ground pepper

Four 6-ounce skinless red snapper fillets

4 SERVINGS | TOTAL: 40 MIN

1 Preheat the broiler. In a large bowl, toss the radishes, fennel, bell pepper, jalapeño, cilantro, chives and mint. Using a sharp knife, peel the grapefruit and orange, removing all of the bitter white pith. Working over the bowl, cut between the membranes and release the sections into the bowl. Squeeze the membranes over the bowl. Add the 2 tablespoons of olive oil and the lemon juice to the bowl and season the salad with salt and pepper.

2 Set the fish on a well-oiled, sturdy baking sheet and brush with olive oil; season with salt and pepper. Broil 6 inches from the heat for 4 minutes, on one side only, just until white throughout. Using a spatula, transfer the fish to plates and serve with the salad.

Sea Bass Fillets *with* Parsley Sauce

Borrowing ingredients from the French classic sole meunière (sole served with browned butter, lemon and parsley), private chef Bob Chambers mixes chopped parsley into bread crumbs to make a coating for sea bass, then fries the fish in butter and olive oil to create a delectable golden crust.

A Sauvignon Blanc from Chile would be terrific with this sea bass. Although they are often overshadowed by Chile's big red Cabernets and Carmenères, the country's Sauvignon Blancs are spectacular; many have more floral and herbal notes than Sauvignons from other regions. Look for the 2009 Lapostolle Casa or the 2009 Viu Manent Secreto.

INGREDIENTS

- 1¾ cups fresh bread crumbs
- 1 cup finely chopped flat-leaf parsley
- Salt and freshly ground pepper
- 4 tablespoons unsalted butter
- 1 shallot, minced
- 1½ cups chicken stock or low-sodium broth
- 3 tablespoons fresh lemon juice
- 3 tablespoons crème fraîche
- ¼ cup extra-virgin olive oil
- All-purpose flour, for dredging
- 2 large eggs, beaten
- Four 6-ounce sea bass fillets

4 SERVINGS | TOTAL: 40 MIN

1 In a large bowl, mix 1½ cups of the bread crumbs with ½ cup of the parsley, 1½ teaspoons of salt and ½ teaspoon of pepper.

2 In a small saucepan, melt 2 tablespoons of the butter. Add the shallot and cook over moderate heat until translucent, about 1 minute. Add the chicken stock and lemon juice and boil over high heat until reduced to 1 cup, about 15 minutes.

3 Whisk the crème fraîche into the sauce along with the remaining ½ cup of parsley and ¼ cup of bread crumbs. Scrape the sauce into a blender and puree. Strain the sauce back into the saucepan and rewarm gently over low heat.

4 In a skillet, melt the remaining 2 tablespoons of butter in the oil over moderate heat. Put the flour and eggs in 2 shallow bowls. Season the sea bass fillets with salt and pepper, then dredge them in flour, dip in the beaten eggs and coat with the bread crumb mixture. When the butter starts to brown slightly, add the fillets to the skillet and cook until browned on the bottom, 3 minutes. Flip the fillets and cook until just white throughout, 2 to 3 minutes longer. Transfer the fish to plates, spoon the sauce alongside and serve.

SAUCE VARIATION **Lemon-Hazelnut Brown Butter** Preheat the oven to 350°. On a baking sheet, toast ½ cup of hazelnuts for 8 minutes, until fragrant. Using a clean kitchen towel, rub the skins off the nuts. Coarsely chop the hazelnuts. In a skillet, cook 4 tablespoons of unsalted butter over moderate heat until browned, about 4 minutes. Add the chopped nuts and 2 tablespoons of fresh lemon juice. Season with salt and pepper and pour over the fish.

FISH VARIATION Striped bass or red snapper.

Striped Bass *with* Caramelized Brussels Sprouts

Although brussels sprouts are usually partnered with poultry or meat, chef Michael Schwartz of Michael's Genuine Food & Drink in Miami likes serving them with fish, such as this pan-roasted striped bass. He cooks the sprouts with pancetta to give them a rich, meaty flavor and accompanies the dish with an easy-to-make garlic aioli amped up with lemon zest.

Most white fish goes best with white or rosé wines, but add pan-roasted brussels sprouts with pancetta and the wine needs more heft. Oregon Pinot Noir's aromatic fruit and moderate tannins make it ideal with this striped bass. Look for the 2008 Erath Oregon or the 2008 Argyle Willamette Valley.

INGREDIENTS

½ cup mayonnaise

¼ cup extra-virgin olive oil

1 garlic clove, minced

½ teaspoon finely grated lemon zest

1 teaspoon fresh lemon juice

Salt and freshly ground pepper

One 3-ounce piece of pancetta, sliced ¼ inch thick and cut into ½-inch pieces

1 pound brussels sprouts, halved lengthwise

2 large thyme sprigs

2 tablespoons vegetable oil

Four 6- to 7-ounce wild striped bass or grouper fillets with skin

Sweet paprika, for garnish

4 SERVINGS | TOTAL: 45 MIN

1 Preheat the oven to 425°. In a small bowl, whisk the mayonnaise with 2 tablespoons of the olive oil and the garlic, lemon zest and lemon juice; season the garlic aioli with salt and pepper.

2 In a large ovenproof skillet, heat the remaining 2 tablespoons of olive oil. Add the pancetta and cook over moderate heat until it is golden and some of the fat has been rendered, about 4 minutes. Add the brussels sprouts, cut side down, and the thyme sprigs. Cook over moderately high heat, without stirring, until the brussels sprouts start to brown, about 4 minutes. Transfer the skillet to the bottom third of the oven and roast for about 10 minutes, until the brussels sprouts are tender and browned all over; discard the thyme sprigs.

3 Meanwhile, in another large ovenproof skillet, heat the vegetable oil until shimmering. Make 3 shallow slashes in the skin of each bass fillet to prevent curling. Season the bass with salt and pepper and add to the skillet, skin side down. Cook over moderately high heat until the skin is browned and crisp, about 4 minutes. Turn the fillets, transfer the skillet to the upper third of the oven and roast for about 4 minutes, until the fish is just white throughout.

4 Transfer the bass to plates and garnish with paprika. Spoon the brussels sprouts alongside; serve right away, with the garlic aioli.

MAKE AHEAD The garlic aioli can be refrigerated overnight.

Sautéed Trout *with* Citrus-Olive Relish

Rather than serving sautéed trout with a refined French lemon-caper pan sauce, chef Clark Frasier of Arrows Restaurant in Ogunquit, Maine, makes a fresh, chunky relish with lemon and oranges—both the sections and the zest—and salty olives in place of the capers.

Australian Riesling has an intriguing lime flavor that gives a zesty kick to seafood dishes like this sautéed trout. Try the 2009 Wolf Blass Gold Label or the 2008 Penfolds Thomas Hyland.

INGREDIENTS

- 2 navel oranges
- 1 small lemon
- 1 teaspoon finely grated orange zest
- ½ teaspoon finely grated lemon zest
- ¼ cup pitted green olives, thinly sliced
- 2 tablespoons chopped parsley

- 1 teaspoon minced garlic
- ¼ cup extra-virgin olive oil
- 2 tablespoons red wine vinegar
- Salt and freshly ground pepper
- 1 tablespoon vegetable oil
- Four 6-ounce skinless trout fillets
- All-purpose flour, for dusting

4 SERVINGS | TOTAL: 25 MIN

1 Using a sharp knife, peel the bitter white pith from the oranges and lemon; be sure to remove all of the pith. Working over a bowl, cut in between the membranes to release the sections. Add the grated orange and lemon zests, olives, parsley, garlic, olive oil and vinegar. Season the relish with salt and pepper and toss gently.

2 In a large nonstick skillet, heat the vegetable oil. Season the trout fillets with salt and pepper and dust with flour. Add the trout to the skillet and cook over moderately high heat until browned on the bottom, about 2 minutes. Turn the fillets, reduce the heat to moderate and cook until just white throughout, about 3 minutes. Transfer the fillets to plates or a platter, spoon the relish on top and serve.

SERVE WITH Quinoa salad.

Crunchy Fish Sticks *with* Tartar Sauce

By adding instant potato flakes to flour, FOOD & WINE's Grace Parisi creates a supercrispy crust for fish sticks. She also updates the tartar sauce with sun-dried tomatoes and cayenne pepper in addition to the usual sweet pickles and lemon juice.

Rich white wines will make fried fish taste heavy. Instead, look for a medium-bodied white Bordeaux blend of Sauvignon Blanc and Sémillon—it'll brighten the seafood just like a squirt of lemon would. Try the 2008 Bridesmaid white from Napa or the 2009 Cape Mentelle Sauvignon Blanc–Sémillon from Australia.

INGREDIENTS

- ½ cup mayonnaise
- 4 oil-packed sun-dried tomatoes, finely chopped
- 3 sweet gherkins, finely chopped
- 2 tablespoons finely chopped red onion
- 2 tablespoons finely chopped dill
- 1 teaspoon fresh lemon juice, plus lemon wedges for serving

- Salt
- Cayenne pepper
- 2 large eggs
- 2 tablespoons water
- ¾ cup all-purpose flour
- 1 cup instant potato flakes
- 1¾ pounds cod fillets, cut into 4-by-¾-inch strips
- Vegetable oil, for frying

6 SERVINGS | TOTAL: 30 MIN

1 In a small bowl, combine the mayonnaise with the sun-dried tomatoes, gherkins, red onion, dill and lemon juice. Season the tartar sauce with salt and cayenne pepper.

2 In a shallow bowl, whisk the eggs with the water. In another shallow bowl, mix ½ cup of the flour with salt and cayenne. In a third shallow bowl, combine the potato flakes with the remaining ¼ cup of flour and season with salt and cayenne. Line a baking sheet with wax paper and another one with paper towels.

3 Working in batches, dredge the cod in the flour, tapping off the excess. Dip the cod in the egg, allow any excess to drip back into the bowl, then coat the cod in the potato flakes, pressing to help them adhere. Transfer the cod to the wax paper–lined baking sheet.

4 In a large, deep skillet, heat 1½ inches of vegetable oil to 325°. Working in 2 batches, fry the cod in the hot oil, turning once, until deep golden and crispy, about 3 minutes. Using a slotted spoon, transfer the fish to the paper towel–lined baking sheet and sprinkle lightly with salt. Repeat with the remaining fish. Serve the fish sticks immediately, with the tartar sauce and lemon wedges.

MAKE AHEAD The tartar sauce can be refrigerated for up to 1 week.

Scallops *with* Potato Pancakes & Caviar Sauce

The combination of potato pancakes and smoked salmon is classic. But the always-irreverent chefs Vinny Dotolo and Jon Shook of Animal restaurant in Los Angeles ingeniously top their potato pancakes with plump seared scallops and a drizzle of Champagne-caviar butter sauce.

Just as Champagne pairs well with caviar, so does sparkling Vouvray, which is a bit richer and fruitier. Two bottles to try with these scallops are the NV François Pinon Vouvray Brut and the NV Champalou Vouvray Pétillant Brut.

INGREDIENTS

PANCAKES
- 1 pound baking potatoes, peeled
- 1 large egg, lightly beaten
- ¼ cup matzo meal
- ¼ cup grated onion
- Salt
- Vegetable oil, for frying

SCALLOPS AND CAVIAR SAUCE
- 1½ cups Champagne
- 9 black peppercorns
- 3 thyme sprigs
- 1 bay leaf
- 1 large shallot, thinly sliced
- 1 teaspoon fresh lemon juice
- 1½ tablespoons crème fraîche
- 1½ sticks (6 ounces) cold unsalted butter, cut into tablespoons
- 1 ounce caviar
- Salt
- Vegetable oil, for frying
- 20 medium sea scallops (1 pound)
- 2 tablespoons minced chives

10 FIRST-COURSE SERVINGS | TOTAL: 1 HR 20 MIN

1 **Make the pancakes** Coarsely shred the potatoes and squeeze out any excess liquid. Transfer to a large bowl and stir in the egg, matzo meal, onion and a large pinch of salt. Shape the mixture into 20 scallop-size cakes about ½ inch thick; press to compress the cakes.

2 In a large skillet, heat ¼ inch of vegetable oil until shimmering. Working in batches, fry the pancakes over moderately high heat until browned and crisp, about 3 minutes per side. Lower the heat if the pancakes brown too quickly and add more oil if necessary. Transfer the pancakes to a baking sheet and sprinkle with salt.

3 **Prepare the scallops and caviar sauce** Preheat the oven to 325°. In a small saucepan, combine the Champagne with the peppercorns, thyme sprigs, bay leaf, shallot and lemon juice and boil over high heat until reduced to 1 tablespoon, about 15 minutes. Strain the sauce into another small saucepan. Stir in the crème fraîche and bring to a simmer over moderate heat. Remove from the heat and stir in the butter, 1 tablespoon at a time. Stir in the caviar and season lightly with salt. Cover the sauce and keep it warm.

4 Wipe out the skillet and heat ¼ inch of oil in it until shimmering. Season the scallops with salt and add half of them to the skillet. Cook over high heat until richly browned, about 1½ minutes per side. Transfer to a plate and keep warm while you cook the remaining scallops.

5 Rewarm the potato pancakes in the oven. Arrange the pancakes on a platter and set a scallop on each one. Add the chives to the caviar butter sauce and spoon over the scallops. Serve right away.

MAKE AHEAD The pancakes and caviar sauce can stand at room temperature for up to 2 hours. Rewarm the caviar sauce over low heat, stirring constantly.

Pretzel-Crusted Crab Cakes

Moving on from bread crumbs, chefs are playing with pretzel crumbs, creating dishes like pretzel-coated chicken, pretzel-coated lamb chops, even pretzel-coated squid. Here, Boston chef Stephanie Sokolove of Stephanie's on Newbury and Stephi's on Tremont uses crushed pretzels to bind and crust chunky crab cakes.

INGREDIENTS

- ½ cup mayonnaise
- 1 large egg
- 1 tablespoon Dijon mustard
- ¼ teaspoon Old Bay seasoning
- ¼ teaspoon sweet paprika
- 3 scallions, green parts only, thinly sliced

- 1 pound lump crabmeat, picked over for shell
- ¾ cup finely ground hard pretzels (from ½ pound pretzels)
- 2 tablespoons unsalted butter
- 1 tablespoon vegetable oil

4 SERVINGS | ACTIVE: 25 MIN; TOTAL: 1 HR 30 MIN

1 In a large bowl, whisk the mayonnaise with the egg, Dijon mustard, Old Bay seasoning, paprika and scallions. Gently fold in the crabmeat and ½ cup of the pretzels. Refrigerate the crab mixture for 1 hour, until the pretzels are moist.

2 Preheat the oven to 400°. Form the crab mixture into eight 2½-inch patties. Coat the crab cakes with the remaining ¼ cup of ground pretzels. In an ovenproof nonstick skillet, melt the butter in the oil. Add the crab cakes and cook over moderately high heat until browned on the bottom, about 3 minutes. Turn the crab cakes and transfer the skillet to the oven. Bake the crab cakes for about 5 minutes, until they are browned all over, then serve.

SERVE WITH Mayonnaise whisked with roasted garlic and mustard.

MAKE AHEAD The crabmeat mixture can be refrigerated overnight.

Many Oregon producers are having success with Pinot Blanc and Pinot Gris, both of which have rich fruit that makes them terrific with these crab cakes. Try the 2008 Pinot Blanc from Elk Cove Vineyards or the 2009 Dundee Hills Pinot Gris from the Four Graces.

Chile-Lime Crab Salad *with* Avocado

Chef Sue Zemanick of Gautreau's in New Orleans updates the classic mix of fresh crab, avocado and tomatoes by tossing her salad with a jalapeño-spiced dressing, then layering it inside glass tumblers with avocado slices and cherry tomatoes to serve as an hors d'oeuvre.

INGREDIENTS

- 5 tablespoons fresh lime juice
- 2½ tablespoons extra-virgin olive oil
- 2½ tablespoons vegetable oil
- 1 tablespoon very finely chopped jalapeño
- 1 tablespoon chopped cilantro
- ½ tablespoon honey
- ½ teaspoon minced garlic

- Salt and freshly ground black pepper
- ½ pound lump crabmeat, picked over for shell
- 2 Hass avocados—1½ cut into ½-inch dice, ½ sliced for garnish
- ⅓ cup minced red onion
- 8 ounces mixed cherry tomatoes, chopped

4 FIRST-COURSE SERVINGS | ☺ | TOTAL: 30 MIN

1 In a small bowl, combine the lime juice with the olive oil, vegetable oil, jalapeño, cilantro, honey and garlic. Season the dressing with salt and pepper.

2 In a small bowl, toss the crab with 3 tablespoons of the dressing and season with salt and pepper. In a medium bowl, gently toss the diced avocado with the red onion and 2 tablespoons of the dressing; season with salt and pepper. In a small bowl, season the cherry tomatoes with salt.

3 Divide the tomatoes among 4 glasses. Top each serving with a quarter of the diced avocado mixture and the crab and garnish with the avocado slices. Drizzle the remaining dressing on top and serve.

Rich crab and avocado call for a white wine with body; at the same time, only a white with good acidity will stand up to the sweet-spicy-tart dressing here. Chardonnays from Sonoma's Russian River Valley and Sonoma Coast appellations would work well. Look for the 2008 Freeman Ryo-fu Chardonnay or the 2007 Gallo of Sonoma Estate.

Crab & Andouille Jambalaya

Creole jambalaya typically features rice and some combination of shrimp, chicken and andouille sausage. To make her more luxurious version, FOOD & WINE's Grace Parisi uses lump crabmeat in place of shrimp and chicken. If she can't find andouille, she opts for more readily available kielbasa.

There are lots of robust, spicy flavors in this jambalaya—from both the andouille and the Old Bay seasoning—so it needs an equally robust red wine. Medium-bodied, fruit-forward Tempranillo from Rioja is a great choice. Look for the 2007 Marqués de Cáceres Rioja Crianza or the 2007 Artadi Viñas de Gain.

INGREDIENTS

- ¼ cup extra-virgin olive oil
- 12 ounces andouille sausage or kielbasa, quartered lengthwise and cut into ¾-inch pieces
- 1 large onion, coarsely chopped
- 1 red bell pepper, finely chopped
- 1 celery rib, finely chopped
- 2 large garlic cloves, minced
- 1 teaspoon Old Bay seasoning
- 1¼ cups jasmine rice (9 ounces)
- 1½ cups chicken stock or low-sodium broth
- 1½ cups water
- 1 thyme sprig
- Salt and freshly ground pepper
- ½ pound lump crabmeat, picked over for shell
- 3 scallions, finely chopped
- Hot sauce, for serving

4 SERVINGS | TOTAL: 40 MIN

1 In a medium enameled cast-iron casserole, heat the olive oil. Add the andouille and cook over high heat, stirring occasionally, until lightly browned, about 3 minutes. Transfer to a bowl.

2 Add the onion, bell pepper, celery and garlic to the casserole. Cover and cook over high heat, stirring occasionally, until the vegetables are softened, about 3 minutes. Add the Old Bay seasoning, rice and andouille and cook, stirring occasionally, until the rice is opaque, about 2 minutes. Add the stock, water and thyme, season lightly with salt and pepper and bring to a boil. Cover and cook over very low heat until the rice is tender and the liquid is absorbed, about 15 minutes. Fluff with a fork and stir in the crab and scallions. Cover and let stand for 2 to 3 minutes, just until the crab is hot; discard the thyme sprig. Serve the jambalaya in bowls, passing hot sauce at the table.

Chipotle Shrimp Tostadas

In this lightened take on a traditional tostada, FOOD & WINE's Melissa Rubel Jacobson replaces steak or chicken with chile-spiced shrimp and switches out salsa for a crisp, citrusy slaw.

INGREDIENTS

1 teaspoon vegetable oil, plus more for frying

4 corn tortillas

Kosher salt

24 shelled and deveined large shrimp (about 1 pound)

1 teaspoon chipotle chile powder

4 cups shredded cabbage or coleslaw mix

1 medium tomato, seeded and cut into ¼-inch dice

2 scallions, thinly sliced

¼ cup sour cream

1½ teaspoons fresh lime juice

1 Hass avocado, thinly sliced

2 medium radishes, thinly sliced

¼ cup cilantro leaves

Lime wedges, for serving

4 SERVINGS | TOTAL: 40 MIN

1 In a medium, deep skillet, heat ¼ inch of vegetable oil until hot. Fry 1 tortilla at a time over moderately high heat until lightly golden on both sides, about 2 minutes. Drain on paper towels and sprinkle with salt.

2 Preheat a grill pan. In a medium bowl, toss the shrimp with the 1 teaspoon of vegetable oil and the chipotle chile powder, then season with salt. Grill the shrimp over moderately high heat, turning once, until browned in spots and cooked through, about 4 minutes.

3 In another medium bowl, toss the cabbage with the tomato, scallions, sour cream and lime juice and season with salt. Set the tortillas on plates and top with the cabbage slaw, chipotle shrimp, avocado, radishes and cilantro. Serve with lime wedges.

Grenache-based rosés are more robust than rosés made with grapes like Pinot Noir. This full-bodied style is especially refreshing with spicy seafood dishes like these tostadas. Look for the 2009 S.C. Pannell Árido from Australia or the 2009 Tres Ojos Rosado from Spain.

Sizzling Shrimp Scampi

Scampi usually refers to shrimp sautéed in garlicky butter or oil or both. FOOD & WINE's Melissa Rubel Jacobson roasts the shrimp in butter spiked with lemon and herbs as well as garlic, then serves the sizzling seafood right from the gratin dish with lots of crusty bread.

INGREDIENTS

- 2 sticks (8 ounces) unsalted butter, softened
- 3 large garlic cloves, very finely chopped
- 1 tablespoon plus 2 teaspoons chopped flat-leaf parsley
- 1½ teaspoons finely grated lemon zest
- 1 teaspoon fresh lemon juice
- ½ teaspoon chopped thyme
- Kosher salt and freshly ground black pepper
- 3 pounds large shrimp, shelled and deveined, tails left on
- 1 tablespoon thinly sliced basil
- Crusty bread, for serving

8 SERVINGS | :) | TOTAL: 30 MIN

1 Preheat the oven to 450°. In a medium bowl, mix the butter with the garlic, 2 teaspoons of the parsley, the lemon zest, lemon juice and thyme and season with salt and pepper.

2 In a large gratin dish, arrange the shrimp, tails up, in a circular pattern. Dot the shrimp with the flavored butter and roast for about 10 minutes, until the shrimp are pink and the butter is bubbling. Sprinkle the shrimp with the remaining 1 tablespoon of chopped parsley and the sliced basil. Serve hot, with crusty bread.

MAKE AHEAD The flavored butter can be refrigerated for up to 1 week or frozen for up to 1 month.

When aged in oak, Chardonnay develops a luscious texture that goes nicely with these buttery shrimp. Try the 2007 Ferrari-Carano Tré Terre or the 2007 Landmark Damaris Reserve.

Sake-Steamed Mussels *with* Ginger & Miso

Mussels steamed in white wine (*moules marinières*) are a French classic. In this Asian-inflected variation, FOOD & WINE's Grace Parisi steams mussels in ginger-infused sake, then flavors the broth with miso—an earthy, slightly salty Japanese paste made from fermented soybeans and rice or barley.

Bold seafood dishes like this call for bold, aromatic whites like Gewürztraminer. The wine often has spicy ginger notes that go well with Asian dishes. Look for the 2007 Trimbach Gewürztraminer from Alsace or the 2008 Navarro Vineyards bottling from California's northern Mendocino region.

INGREDIENTS

- 4 thick slices of white peasant bread
- ¼ cup extra-virgin olive oil, plus more for brushing
- 2 garlic cloves—1 left whole, 1 thinly sliced
- 1 medium shallot, minced
- 2 tablespoons very finely chopped fresh ginger
- Salt and freshly ground pepper

- 4 pounds mussels, scrubbed and debearded
- 1½ cups dry sake
- 4 tablespoons unsalted butter, at room temperature
- 2 tablespoons white miso
- 2 tablespoons coarsely chopped flat-leaf parsley
- 2 tablespoons coarsely chopped cilantro

4 SERVINGS | TOTAL: 20 MIN

1 Preheat the broiler. Brush the bread with olive oil and transfer to a baking sheet. Broil the bread a few inches from the heat, turning once, for 2 minutes, until golden and toasted. Lightly rub the whole garlic clove over the toasts.

2 In a large, deep pot, heat the ¼ cup of olive oil. Add the minced shallot, sliced garlic and chopped ginger, season lightly with salt and pepper and cook over high heat, stirring, until the garlic is softened and lightly browned, about 3 minutes. Add the mussels and cook, stirring, for 1 minute. Add the sake, cover and steam the mussels until they open, about 5 minutes. Remove the pot from the heat. Using a slotted spoon, transfer the mussels to 4 deep bowls, discarding any mussels that do not open.

3 Add the butter, miso, parsley and cilantro to the broth, swirling and shaking the pot until the butter melts. Slowly pour the broth over the mussels, stopping before you reach the grit at the bottom of the pot. Serve the mussels with the garlic toasts.

Poultry

Chicken Drumsticks *with* Asian Barbecue Sauce

Instead of looking to Kansas City or the Carolinas for barbecue sauce inspiration, FOOD & WINE's Grace Parisi prepares a sweet, sticky, slightly fiery version using Asian ingredients like hoisin sauce and ginger. She coats the drumsticks with salt, pepper and Chinese five-spice powder and roasts them; then she brushes them with the sweet-spicy sauce and broils until crispy.

Argentina's Malbec offers terrific bang for the buck, and its juicy berry fruit makes it a great partner for the spicy barbecue sauce on these drumsticks. Two good choices: the 2007 Trapiche Broquel and the 2007 Navarro Correas Colección Privada.

INGREDIENTS

- 2 tablespoons vegetable oil
- 1 teaspoon Chinese five-spice powder
- 16 chicken drumsticks (3 pounds)
- Salt and freshly ground pepper
- ¾ cup hoisin sauce
- ¼ cup sweet Asian chile sauce or hot pepper jelly
- ¼ cup unseasoned rice vinegar
- ¼ cup chicken stock or broth
- 2 tablespoons minced fresh ginger
- 2 large garlic cloves
- 1 teaspoon toasted sesame oil
- 1 cup toasted sesame seeds

8 SERVINGS | ACTIVE: 20 MIN; TOTAL: 1 HR

1 Preheat the oven to 425°. In a large bowl, mix the vegetable oil with the five-spice powder. Add the chicken, season with salt and pepper and toss. Arrange the chicken on a foil-lined baking sheet. Roast for about 35 minutes, turning twice, until cooked.

2 Meanwhile, in a blender, combine the hoisin sauce, chile sauce, rice vinegar, chicken stock, ginger, garlic and sesame oil and puree until very smooth. Transfer the sauce to a saucepan and simmer until slightly thickened, 5 minutes.

3 Transfer the chicken to a large bowl and toss with the sauce until completely coated.

4 Preheat the broiler and position a rack 8 inches from the heat. Return the chicken to the baking sheet and broil for about 10 minutes, brushing with the sauce and turning occasionally, until the chicken is glazed and sticky.

5 Add the toasted sesame seeds to a small bowl. Dip the chicken in the seeds to coat and serve.

Chicken *with* Apricot-Onion Pan Sauce

Whole dried apricots and apricot jam aren't typical sauce ingredients (except in desserts), but FOOD & WINE's Melissa Rubel Jacobson uses them in this clever, easy chicken recipe. After sautéing the breasts, she adds diced onion and white wine to sweep up the crispy browned bits left in the skillet, then sweetens the sauce slightly with the dried fruit and preserves.

Full-bodied California Viogniers often have a peachy aroma that makes them ideal with fruity sauces. Pour the 2008 Bonterra Vineyards or the 2008 Alban Vineyards Central Coast.

INGREDIENTS

3½ ounces dried apricots

4 boneless chicken breasts with skin (9 ounces each)

Salt and freshly ground pepper

1 tablespoon olive oil

1 large onion, diced

1 garlic clove, thinly sliced

2 thyme sprigs

1 bay leaf

½ cup dry white wine

1½ cups chicken stock

2 tablespoons apricot preserves

1 tablespoon unsalted butter

4 SERVINGS | :) | TOTAL: 35 MIN

1 Preheat the oven to 350°. In a bowl, cover the apricots with hot water and let stand until soft, about 15 minutes; drain.

2 Meanwhile, dry the chicken with paper towels and season with salt and pepper. In a stainless steel skillet, heat the oil. Add the chicken, skin side down, and cook over moderately high heat until golden brown, 5 minutes. Flip and cook about 3 minutes longer. Transfer the chicken to a baking sheet and roast for about 14 minutes.

3 Add the onion, garlic, thyme sprigs and bay leaf to the skillet. Season with salt and cook over moderate heat until the onion is tender. Add the wine and boil until reduced by half, scraping up the browned bits in the skillet. Add the chicken stock, apricots and apricot preserves and bring to a boil. Cook over high heat until the sauce thickens. Off the heat, swirl in the butter until melted. Discard the thyme sprigs and bay leaf. Season the sauce with salt and pepper. Transfer the chicken to plates, spoon the sauce on top and serve.

Thai Green Curry Chicken Wings

Spicy chicken wings (a.k.a. buffalo wings or hot wings) are a classic American snack. In this version—which takes only 15 minutes of prep time—FOOD & WINE's Grace Parisi puts an Asian spin on the dish, replacing red hot sauce with green and adding fish sauce, cilantro and Thai green curry paste.

INGREDIENTS

- 2 tablespoons all-purpose flour
- 1 teaspoon salt
- 1 teaspoon ground coriander
- 2 pounds chicken wingettes and drumettes (see Note)
- 2½ tablespoons green hot sauce

- 2 tablespoons unsalted butter, melted
- ½ tablespoon fish sauce
- 1 teaspoon Thai green curry paste
- 2 tablespoons chopped cilantro

2 TO 4 SERVINGS | ACTIVE: 15 MIN; TOTAL: 1 HR

1 Preheat the oven to 500°. Line a large baking sheet with aluminum foil and spray with vegetable oil. In a large bowl, mix the flour with the salt and coriander. Add the chicken and toss to coat. Spread the chicken on the baking sheet in a single layer and spray with vegetable oil. Roast the chicken for about 45 minutes, turning once or twice, until browned and crispy.

2 In a large bowl, whisk the green hot sauce with the butter, fish sauce and green curry paste. Add the chicken wings and toss. Sprinkle with the chopped cilantro and serve.

NOTE Wingettes and drumettes are often sold separately.

Nothing goes better with hot wings than cold beer. Try a crisp lager like Samuel Adams Boston Lager or the caramelly Blue Point Toasted Lager.

Sour-Orange Yucatán Chicken

Cooks in Mexico's Yucatán use deep red annatto paste (typically sold as achiote paste) to season chicken, pork and fish. FOOD & WINE's Marcia Kiesel replaces the ground annatto seeds with paprika; it's easier to find, and she thinks it tastes better, too. She then adds fresh citrus juices, cumin, ancho chile powder and 20 cloves of garlic to make a terrifically spicy rub for whole roast chicken.

✳ *There are essentially two styles of Sauvignon Blanc: the grassy, herbal version and the citrusy, tropical variety. One of the latter will go well with this vibrant chicken, like the 2009 Charles Krug Napa Valley or the 2008 Star Lane Vineyard Sauvignon Blanc.*

INGREDIENTS

- 20 garlic cloves, halved
- ¼ cup vegetable oil
- 1⅓ cups fresh orange juice
- ½ cup fresh lemon juice
- ¼ cup pure ancho chile powder
- 2 tablespoons hot paprika
- 4 teaspoons kosher salt, plus more for seasoning
- 2 teaspoons ground cumin
- Two 3½-pound chickens
- ¼ cup plus 1 tablespoon honey

8 SERVINGS
ACTIVE: 40 MIN; TOTAL: 3 HR PLUS OVERNIGHT MARINATING

1 In a food processor, mince the garlic with the vegetable oil. Add the orange and lemon juices, chile powder, paprika, 4 teaspoons of salt and the cumin and blend well.

2 Loosen the skin on the chicken breasts and around the legs. Put each chicken in a bowl and cover with the marinade. Rub the marinade under the skin and in the cavity. Turn the chickens breast side up and refrigerate overnight.

3 Preheat the oven to 350°. Set the chickens breast side up in a large roasting pan and season with salt. Add the marinade to the pan along with 1 cup of water. Bake for 1 hour. Spoon ¼ cup of the pan juices into a small bowl and stir in 3 tablespoons of the honey; pour over the chickens and bake for about 1 hour and 15 minutes, until an instant-read thermometer inserted in the inner thighs registers 160°.

4 Drain the cavity juices into the roasting pan. Transfer the chickens to a carving board to rest for 10 minutes. Pour the pan juices into a saucepan. Add the remaining 2 tablespoons of honey, bring to a boil and season with salt. Carve the chickens and serve with the sauce.

Grilled-Chicken Tacos

Pureed tomatoes are the secret to this fantastically simple chicken marinade from brothers Leo and Oliver Kremer and chef Miguel Franco of New York City's Dos Toros Taqueria. After steeping overnight in a mixture of pureed tomatoes, lime juice, water and salt, the chicken in these tacos is so juicy and delicious, it needs only a light sprinkling of cheese, avocado and other toppings.

The smokiness of this grilled chicken suggests a red wine pairing. Choose a fruity, medium-bodied California Pinot Noir like the 2008 Cellar No. 8, a blend from several appellations, or the 2008 Poppy from Monterey.

INGREDIENTS

- 3 medium tomatoes, coarsely chopped
- ⅓ cup fresh lime juice
- 1 cup water
- 1 teaspoon salt
- 2 pounds skinless, boneless chicken thighs
- 2 tablespoons vegetable oil
- 1 teaspoon sweet paprika
- 1 teaspoon dried parsley
- 12 corn tortillas, warmed
- Shredded Monterey Jack cheese, jarred salsa verde and chopped avocados, onions, tomatoes and cilantro, for serving

MAKES 12 TACOS | TOTAL: 30 MIN PLUS 6 HR MARINATING

1 In a blender, puree the coarsely chopped tomatoes with the lime juice, water and salt. Transfer the puree to a large resealable plastic bag and add the chicken thighs. Seal the bag, pressing out the air. Refrigerate the chicken for 6 hours or overnight.

2 Light a grill or preheat a grill pan. Remove the chicken thighs from the marinade and pat them dry. Brush with the oil and sprinkle with the paprika and parsley. Grill over moderately high heat, turning occasionally, until the chicken is lightly charred and cooked through, about 15 minutes. Transfer the chicken to a work surface and let stand for 5 minutes. Cut the chicken into strips and serve with the warmed tortillas, cheese, salsa verde, avocados, onions, tomatoes and cilantro.

MAKE AHEAD The grilled chicken can be refrigerated overnight.

Chinese Chicken Salad *with* Oranges

Chinese chicken salad is an American invention that's chopped, heavily dressed and liberally sprinkled with fried chow mein noodles. For her light and easy version of the salad, chef Joanne Chang of Flour bakery and café in Boston tosses store-bought rotisserie chicken, roasted peanuts, scallions and celery with a salty-spicy-sweet dressing, then serves the salad over whole romaine leaves. She sometimes makes the recipe even crunchier by adding napa cabbage, cucumbers and carrots.

INGREDIENTS

¼ cup mayonnaise

¼ cup plus 2 tablespoons unseasoned rice vinegar

3 tablespoons plus 1½ teaspoons sugar

¼ cup soy sauce

2 tablespoons toasted sesame oil

1 tablespoon Tabasco

One ½-inch piece of fresh ginger, peeled and minced

1 small garlic clove, minced

One 2½-pound rotisserie chicken, meat shredded, skin and bones reserved for stock or discarded

3 scallions, thinly sliced

2 celery ribs, thinly sliced

1 cup unsalted roasted peanuts, coarsely chopped

¾ cup coarsely chopped cilantro

1 small head of romaine, separated

1 tablespoon extra-virgin olive oil

2 oranges, peeled with a knife and cut into sections

Lime wedges, for serving

4 SERVINGS | :) | TOTAL: 35 MIN

1 In a large bowl, whisk the mayonnaise with ¼ cup of the vinegar, 3 tablespoons of the sugar and the soy sauce, sesame oil, Tabasco, ginger and garlic. Add the chicken, scallions, celery, peanuts and cilantro and toss until coated.

2 In another bowl, toss the romaine with the remaining 2 tablespoons of vinegar, 1½ teaspoons of sugar and the olive oil. Arrange the romaine leaves in 4 shallow bowls. Top with the chicken salad and the oranges and serve with lime wedges.

No matter where it's from, Gewürztraminer tends to have aromas that evoke baking spices, flowers and lychee—all of which are great with Asian-style dishes like this cool salad. Try the 2009 Handley from California or the 2008 Helfrich from Alsace.

Herb-Marinated Chicken Skewers

Chef Andres Barrera of City Winery in New York City serves these simple kebabs with two unexpected accompaniments: a fiery harissa (Tunisian chile paste) and a cool chickpea puree. His homemade harissa is a knockout, but the jarred kind is good here, too.

These flavorful chicken skewers go best with a bold wine. The Sonoma Coast produces some of California's best Pinot Noirs, thanks to a cool climate that helps grapes ripen slowly, developing deep, rich berry flavors. Look for the 2008 Hirsch Vineyards Bohan-Dillon or the 2008 La Crema Sonoma Coast.

INGREDIENTS

CHICKEN
- ¼ cup extra-virgin olive oil
- 1 tablespoon rosemary leaves
- 1 teaspoon chopped thyme
- 1 teaspoon chopped oregano
- 1 teaspoon ground cumin
- 1½ pounds skinless, boneless chicken breast halves, cut into 1½-inch cubes

Salt

HARISSA
- 1 teaspoon cumin seeds
- 1 teaspoon coriander seeds
- 1 teaspoon caraway seeds
- 2 roasted red peppers from a jar, coarsely chopped
- 1 red Thai chile, with seeds, chopped
- 1 garlic clove, chopped
- 3 tablespoons extra-virgin olive oil
- 1 tablespoon fresh lemon juice

Salt

Hummus, for serving

4 SERVINGS | TOTAL: 45 MIN PLUS 2 HR MARINATING

1 ***Marinate the chicken*** In a large bowl, mix the olive oil with the rosemary, thyme, oregano and ground cumin. Add the chicken and toss well. Cover and refrigerate for at least 2 hours or overnight.

2 ***Meanwhile, make the harissa*** In a small skillet, toast the cumin, coriander and caraway seeds over moderately high heat, shaking the skillet a few times, until the spices are fragrant, about 2 minutes. Transfer to a spice grinder and let cool completely. Grind to a powder.

3 In a blender, combine the roasted peppers with the chile, garlic, olive oil, lemon juice and ground spices and puree until smooth. Season the harissa with salt.

4 Light a grill. Thread the chicken pieces onto 8 skewers. Season with salt and grill over moderately high heat, turning, until nicely charred and just cooked, about 14 minutes. Serve the grilled skewers with the harissa and hummus.

MAKE AHEAD The harissa can be refrigerated for up to 5 days. Bring to room temperature before serving.

Chicken Hot Pot *with* Mushrooms & Tofu

Cooks in Asia serve hot pots family-style, setting a big container of bubbling broth on the table alongside a platter of raw ingredients (like vegetables and thinly sliced chicken) for dipping. In his version, chef Ethan Stowell of Staple & Fancy Mercantile in Seattle gives each guest a bowl of sliced mushrooms, tofu and scallions, then adds piping hot broth loaded with chunks of tender cooked chicken.

Brothy soups go best with clean, unoaked white wines. A Chardonnay like the 2009 Ruffino Libaio or the 2008 A to Z will have enough weight to go with the umami flavors in this hot pot.

INGREDIENTS

- 12 cups chicken stock or low-sodium broth
- 1 pound honshimeji or cremini mushrooms, stems removed and reserved, caps thinly sliced
- One 2-inch piece of ginger, thinly sliced
- 2 large garlic cloves, crushed
- Kosher salt

- 6 skinless, boneless chicken thighs (about 1¾ pounds), trimmed and sliced into ¼-inch strips
- One 14-ounce package firm tofu, drained and cut into ½-inch dice
- 4 scallions, thinly sliced
- Toasted sesame oil, for drizzling

8 SERVINGS | ACTIVE: 20 MIN; TOTAL: 1 HR

1 In a large soup pot, bring the stock, mushroom stems, ginger and garlic to a simmer. Cook over low heat for 30 minutes. Strain the stock into a bowl and return it to the pot. Season the broth with salt.

2 Bring the broth to a boil; add the chicken. Cook until the chicken is white throughout, about 4 minutes. Divide the mushroom caps, tofu and scallions among 8 soup bowls and serve, passing the broth and sesame oil at the table.

MAKE AHEAD The enriched broth can be refrigerated for up to 3 days.

Chicken Tikka

To make authentic chicken tikka, cooks in India marinate chicken pieces in yogurt and spices, chiefly garam masala (an aromatic blend), then grill them on skewers. In this unskewered version, chef Vikram Sunderam of Rasika in Washington, DC, creates a wonderfully savory marinade using Chinese five-spice powder in place of the garam masala. In addition to including yogurt in the marinade, he uses it to make a cooling cilantro-flavored dipping sauce that comes together instantly in a blender.

As a partner for this spiced chicken, consider Verdejo, one of the most underappreciated white wines in the world, from Spain's central Rueda region. The 2008 Belondrade y Lurton and the 2008 Shaya Old Vines are full-bodied, with vibrant fruit and nice acidity—perfect for this equally bold dish.

INGREDIENTS

- 1 tablespoon mustard seeds
- 1 teaspoon Chinese five-spice powder
- 1 teaspoon freshly ground black pepper
- 1 teaspoon turmeric
- 1 teaspoon cayenne pepper
- 1 bay leaf
- 2 tablespoons minced fresh ginger
- 4 garlic cloves, minced
- 1 cup plain whole-milk yogurt

Kosher salt

- 2 pounds skinless, boneless chicken thighs, cut into 2- to 3-inch pieces
- 2 tablespoons unsalted butter, melted

Cilantro & Yogurt Sauce (recipe follows), for serving

4 TO 6 SERVINGS | ACTIVE: 30 MIN; TOTAL: 2 HR 30 MIN

1 In a spice grinder, pulse the mustard seeds with the five-spice powder, black pepper, turmeric, cayenne and bay leaf until fine. Transfer the spice powder to a medium bowl. Add the ginger, garlic and yogurt and season with salt. Add the chicken and turn to coat. Refrigerate for 2 hours.

2 Light a grill. Remove the chicken from the marinade and brush the pieces with the melted butter. Season with salt. Oil the grate and grill the chicken over high heat, turning occasionally, until lightly charred and cooked through, about 8 minutes. Serve the chicken right away, with the Cilantro & Yogurt Sauce.

SERVE WITH Carrot sticks and warm naan.

MAKE AHEAD The chicken can be marinated for up to 8 hours.

Cilantro & Yogurt Sauce

- 2 cups cilantro leaves
- 1 cup mint leaves
- 1 jalapeño, seeded and coarsely chopped
- 4 garlic cloves, crushed
- 1 teaspoon ground cumin
- 1 tablespoon fresh lemon juice
- 1 cup plain whole-milk yogurt

Kosher salt

MAKES 1½ CUPS | ☺ | TOTAL: 15 MIN

In a blender, combine the cilantro, mint, jalapeño, garlic, cumin and lemon juice and puree to a paste. Add the yogurt and puree until smooth. Season with salt.

MAKE AHEAD The sauce can be refrigerated for up to 2 days.

Skillet Chicken & Mushroom Potpie

FOOD & WINE's Grace Parisi updates chicken potpie with this one-skillet remix prepared with store-bought rotisserie chicken and—her stroke of brilliance—buttered white bread in place of the usual labor-intensive puff pastry crust.

Beaujolais, made with the Gamay grape, is light- to medium-bodied and low in tannins; it's flexible enough to pair with all kinds of dishes, including this earthy potpie. Pour the 2008 Château Thivin Côte de Brouilly or the 2008 Georges Duboeuf Morgon.

INGREDIENTS

- 4 tablespoons unsalted butter, softened
- 1 onion, finely chopped
- ½ pound shiitake mushrooms, stems discarded and caps thinly sliced
- 2 carrots, thinly sliced

Salt and freshly ground pepper

- 3 tablespoons all-purpose flour
- 1 teaspoon sweet paprika
- 1 cup chicken stock or low-sodium broth
- 2 tablespoons Madeira
- 2 cups whole milk
- 3 cups shredded chicken (from a rotisserie chicken)
- ½ cup frozen baby peas

Eight 1-inch-thick slices of bakery white country bread (about 1 pound), crusts removed

6 SERVINGS | TOTAL: 45 MIN

1 Preheat the oven to 425°. In a large ovenproof nonstick skillet, melt 2 tablespoons of the butter. Add the onion, mushrooms and carrots and season lightly with salt and pepper. Cover and cook over high heat, stirring once, until the vegetables are just softened, about 1 minute. Uncover and cook, stirring frequently, until lightly browned, about 5 minutes. Stir in the flour and paprika and cook, stirring, for 1 minute. Add the stock and Madeira and cook, stirring, until blended. Add the milk and bring to a gentle boil. Stir in the chicken and peas and season with salt and pepper. Remove from the heat.

2 Arrange the bread over the chicken mixture, trimming it to fit snugly in a single layer. Brush the bread with the remaining 2 tablespoons of butter. Bake for about 20 minutes, until the filling is bubbling and the bread is golden. Serve right away.

Herb-Roasted Turkey *with* Gravy

"I wasn't always a briner," says Shawn McClain, chef-partner at Sage in Las Vegas. "But when enough people tell you it's the thing to do, you try it." He opts here to both brine the bird and rub it with a buttery herb mixture. The brine—an intriguing combination of fennel, mustard and coriander seeds, plus salt, sugar and water—seasons the meat perfectly and keeps the turkey moist in the oven. The herb coating becomes a sensationally flavorful crust.

Pinot Noir's balance of crisp fruit, light spiciness and moderate tannins makes it very versatile and terrific with this herb-rubbed turkey. Look for the 2006 Fiddlehead Cellars Seven Twenty Eight or the 2008 Ponzi Vineyards Tavola.

INGREDIENTS

- 2 tablespoons fennel seeds
- 2 tablespoons mustard seeds
- 2 tablespoons coriander seeds
- 6 bay leaves
- 1½ cups kosher salt
- 1 cup sugar
- 8 quarts cold water

One 18-pound turkey

- 2 sticks plus 2 tablespoons unsalted butter, softened
- 3 tablespoons chopped parsley
- 1 tablespoon chopped sage
- 1 tablespoon chopped thyme

Freshly ground pepper

- 2 tablespoons all-purpose flour
- 3 quarts chicken stock or low-sodium broth
- ½ small onion, finely chopped
- 1 small carrot, finely chopped
- 1 celery rib, finely chopped
- 1 cup diced peasant bread

12 SERVINGS
ACTIVE: 1 HR; TOTAL: 4 HR 30 MIN PLUS OVERNIGHT BRINING

1 In a large saucepan, combine the fennel, mustard and coriander seeds with the bay leaves, salt, sugar and 1 quart of the water. Bring to a boil, stirring to dissolve the salt and sugar; transfer to a very large bowl or pot and add the remaining water. Add the turkey, breast side down. Cover and refrigerate for at least 8 hours or overnight.

2 Preheat the oven to 450°. Drain and rinse the turkey and pat dry; discard the brine. Use your hand to loosen the turkey skin.

3 In a medium bowl, combine the 2 sticks of butter with the parsley, sage and thyme and season with pepper. Spoon ¼ cup of the herb butter into a bowl and stir in the flour; cover and chill. Spread the remaining herb butter all over and under the skin of the turkey and set it on a rack in a roasting pan. Add 2 cups of the stock to the pan and roast for 30 minutes. Lower the oven to 325° and roast the turkey for about 2½ hours longer, basting occasionally, until an instant-read thermometer inserted in the thigh registers 170°. Transfer the turkey to a cutting board and let rest for 30 minutes.

4 Meanwhile, in a large saucepan, melt the remaining 2 tablespoons of butter. Add the onion, carrot and celery and cook over moderate heat, stirring occasionally, until softened, 5 minutes. Stir in the bread and cook for 1 minute. Add 2 quarts of the stock and bring to a boil. Simmer over moderate heat until reduced to 3 cups, about 1 hour and 15 minutes. Whisk to break up the bread. Strain the stock and return it to the saucepan. Whisk in the chilled herb butter and bring to a boil. Cook, whisking, until thickened, about 5 minutes.

5 Pour off the fat from the roasting pan; place the pan over high heat. Add the remaining stock and cook, scraping up any browned bits, until boiling. Strain the pan drippings into the gravy; season with salt and pepper. Carve the turkey and serve, passing the gravy.

Meat

Peppered Beef Tenderloin

Steak and herb butter is a classic pairing. Chris Lilly of Big Bob Gibson Bar-B-Q in Decatur, Alabama, transforms the dish. First, he rubs the meat with an intriguing mix of black pepper, brown sugar, olive oil, soy sauce and vinegar and wraps each steak individually in plastic so it really soaks up the flavorings. Then he mashes roasted garlic as well as herbs into the butter.

New Zealand Syrahs have a black-pepper note that's perfect with this tenderloin. For a long time, New Zealand exported mostly Pinot Noirs and Sauvignon Blancs to the U.S., but luckily, more and more of its terrific Syrahs are making their way here. Two great ones are the 2008 Man O'War and the 2008 Craggy Range Gimblett Gravels Vineyard.

INGREDIENTS

- 2 tablespoons coarsely ground black pepper
- 1 teaspoon kosher salt
- 1 teaspoon dark brown sugar
- 1 teaspoon soy sauce
- ½ teaspoon apple cider vinegar
- 1 tablespoon plus 1 teaspoon extra-virgin olive oil
- 6 tenderloin steaks (about 1½ inches thick)
- 4 garlic cloves, unpeeled
- ¼ teaspoon each fresh thyme, rosemary and oregano leaves
- 4 tablespoons unsalted butter, softened

6 SERVINGS | ACTIVE: 30 MIN; TOTAL: 1 HR 40 MIN

1 Preheat the oven to 275°. In a small bowl, mix the pepper, salt, brown sugar, soy sauce, vinegar and 1 teaspoon of the olive oil. Rub 2 teaspoons of the paste all over each steak. Wrap the steaks individually in plastic and let stand at room temperature for 1 hour.

2 Meanwhile, on a double-layer square of aluminum foil, drizzle the garlic with the remaining 1 tablespoon of oil. Fold the foil to enclose the garlic and transfer to a baking sheet. Roast for 45 minutes, until the garlic is very soft.

3 When the garlic is cool, squeeze the cloves from their skins into a bowl; add the herbs. Using a fork, mash the garlic with the herbs and butter. Spoon the garlic butter onto a sheet of plastic wrap, roll into a log and refrigerate until firm, 30 minutes.

4 Build a very hot fire on one side of a charcoal grill or light a gas grill. Unwrap each steak and grill over high heat for about 7 minutes, turning once, for rare meat. For medium-rare, transfer the steaks to the cool side of the grill, close the lid and cook for 4 minutes longer, turning them once halfway through. Top the steaks with the garlic-herb butter and let stand for 5 minutes, then serve. **SERVE WITH** Wilted Swiss chard.

Beef Rib Roast *with* Horseradish *&* Herb Crust

Instead of serving a traditional rib roast with horseradish on the side, star chef John Besh of August in New Orleans smears the beef with a paste of horseradish, garlic, herbs and butter, which bakes to form an incredible crust.

INGREDIENTS

- 2 sticks (8 ounces) unsalted butter, softened
- 1 head of garlic, cloves coarsely chopped
- 1 cup prepared horseradish
- ¼ cup plus 2 tablespoons chopped thyme
- 3 tablespoons chopped rosemary
- 3 tablespoons chopped sage
- One 16-pound rib roast of beef
- Salt and freshly ground pepper

12 SERVINGS | ACTIVE: 20 MIN; TOTAL: 4 HR 15 MIN

1 Preheat the oven to 325°. In a food processor, combine the softened butter with the garlic, horseradish and chopped thyme, rosemary and sage. Process the mixture to a paste.

2 Stand the roast in a very large roasting pan. Season generously all over with salt and pepper and set it fatty side up. Spread the horseradish-herb butter all over the top. Cook for about 3½ hours, until an instant-read thermometer inserted in the center registers 125° for medium-rare. Transfer the roast to a carving board to rest for at least 20 minutes or up to 1 hour before serving.

MAKE AHEAD The horseradish-herb butter can be refrigerated overnight. Let the butter soften before using.

With its brawny, firm tannins and slight herbal edge, Cabernet is a good partner for substantial cuts of meat like this rich, herb-crusted rib roast. The 2007 vintage was a spectacular one for California Cabernet. Proof: the 2007 Robert Mondavi Winery Napa Valley and the 2007 Provenance Vineyards Rutherford.

Spice-Rubbed Rib Eyes *with* Lime Butter

Arizona chef Bernie Kantak gives ordinary rib eye steaks an intense Southwest flavor by spicing them with chipotle, cumin and paprika. But the best part is the inspired topping: a puckery lime butter that melts into the juicy grilled beef.

INGREDIENTS

- 4 tablespoons unsalted butter, softened
- 1 small garlic clove, minced
- ¼ teaspoon finely grated lime zest
- 1 tablespoon fresh lime juice
- Kosher salt

- 1½ teaspoons sweet paprika
- 1½ teaspoons ground cumin
- 1½ teaspoons chipotle powder
- Four 12-ounce boneless rib eye steaks (1 inch thick)
- Vegetable oil, for the grill

4 SERVINGS | TOTAL: 30 MIN

1 Light a grill or preheat a grill pan. In a small bowl, combine the butter with the garlic, lime zest, lime juice and a pinch of salt. In another small bowl, combine the paprika, cumin and chipotle powder with 1½ teaspoons of salt. Rub the spice mixture all over the steaks.

2 Oil the grate and grill the steaks over moderately high heat, turning once, until slightly charred and medium-rare, about 12 minutes. Transfer the steaks to plates and top with the lime butter. Let the steaks stand for 3 to 4 minutes before serving.

Malbec from Argentina (a meat-loving country) goes well with steak; its floral aroma makes it particularly good with this spice-rubbed beef. Try the 2008 Catena or, from star California winemaker Paul Hobbs, the 2008 Viña Cobos Bramare Luján de Cuyo.

Grilled Flank Steak *with* Summer Vegetables

To make a dish that's lighter and healthier than the usual steak and potatoes, chef Mark Fuller of Seattle's Spring Hill marinates flank steak (a lean cut) in red wine, slices it thinly and serves it with a seasonal tomato-and-asparagus salad that's good enough to stand on its own as a first course.

For meat with sweet-spicy rubs or marinades, pour similarly spicy, fruit-driven reds, like Argentinean Malbec or Petite Sirah from California. Two good choices are the 2008 BenMarco Malbec and the 2007 Greg Norman Paso Robles Petite Sirah.

INGREDIENTS

1½ cups dry red wine

½ cup Dijon mustard

¼ cup packed dark brown sugar

8 garlic cloves, crushed and peeled

3 large shallots, coarsely chopped

2 tablespoons chopped flat-leaf parsley

1 tablespoon chopped thyme

Kosher salt and freshly ground pepper

One 1½-pound flank steak

2 tablespoons cider vinegar

1 tablespoon honey

6 ounces cherry tomatoes, preferably Sweet 100 tomatoes, quartered (about 1½ cups)

¼ small sweet onion, such as Walla Walla, thinly sliced

6 ounces thin asparagus

2 ears of corn, shucked

1 tablespoon extra-virgin olive oil

6 basil leaves, finely shredded

1 tablespoon unsalted butter

6 ounces fresh morel mushrooms, cleaned and halved if large, or a scant ½ ounce dried morels, reconstituted in boiling water for 10 minutes

---

4 SERVINGS | ACTIVE: 50 MIN; TOTAL: 2 HR 30 MIN

1 In a large glass baking dish, whisk the red wine, mustard, brown sugar, garlic, shallots, parsley, thyme, 1 tablespoon of salt and 1 teaspoon of pepper. Add the steak and turn to coat. Let stand at room temperature for 2 hours or refrigerate for up to 8 hours.

2 Meanwhile, in a medium bowl, whisk the cider vinegar and honey. Add the tomatoes and onion and toss. Let stand for 1 hour.

3 Light a grill. Coat the asparagus and corn with the olive oil and season with salt and pepper. Grill over moderately high heat, turning occasionally, until tender and browned in spots, about 3 minutes for the asparagus and 6 minutes for the corn. Transfer to a work surface. When the vegetables are cool enough to handle, use a vegetable peeler to shave the asparagus into slices and a sharp knife to cut the corn from the cobs. Add the asparagus, corn and basil to the tomatoes; toss.

4 Remove the steak from the marinade and pat dry with paper towels; season lightly with salt and pepper. Grill the steak, turning once, until medium-rare, about 10 minutes total. Transfer the steak to a work surface and let rest for 10 minutes.

5 Meanwhile, in a skillet, melt the butter. Add the morels and cook over moderately high heat until browned, about 3 minutes. Season with salt and pepper.

6 Thinly slice the steak against the grain and transfer to plates. Season the vegetables with salt and pepper and spoon alongside the steak. Top the steak with the morels and serve.

Korean Beef Stew *with* Napa Cabbage & Pickles

When FOOD & WINE's Marcia Kiesel set out to create a recipe for this exceptional Korean classic, she made sure the ingredients were easy to find in a U.S. supermarket: In place of Korean hot peppers and sweet Korean pickles, the stew gets tanginess and heat from jalapeños and sour dill pickles.

This succulent beef would pair well with a soft, rich red like Merlot. Washington State produces some of the best Merlots in the country, such as the 2007 L'Ecole No. 41 Columbia Valley and the 2007 Seven Hills Seven Hills Vineyard from Walla Walla.

INGREDIENTS

- 1 tablespoon vegetable oil
- 3 pounds trimmed beef chuck, cut into 3-inch pieces
- Salt and freshly ground pepper
- ¼ cup soy sauce
- ¼ cup sugar
- ¼ cup dry white wine
- 1 quart beef stock or low-sodium broth
- 2 medium red onions, quartered through the core
- 6 large garlic cloves, coarsely chopped
- 2 large jalapeños—halved, seeded and sliced ½ inch thick
- 2 cups mung bean sprouts
- 1 tablespoon cornstarch
- 4 cups coarsely chopped napa cabbage
- ½ cup thinly sliced sour dill pickles
- Steamed short-grain rice, toasted sesame oil and 3 thinly sliced scallions, for serving

6 SERVINGS | ACTIVE: 30 MIN; TOTAL: 3 HR 40 MIN

1 In a very large skillet, heat the vegetable oil. Season the meat with salt and pepper and sear the pieces over moderately high heat until richly browned all over. Transfer the meat to a large slow cooker, turn it to high and cover.

2 Wipe out the skillet and return it to the burner. Add the soy sauce, sugar, wine and stock and bring to a boil. Pour the mixture into the slow cooker. Add the onions, cover and cook for 2 hours. Add the garlic and jalapeños to the stew, cover and cook for 1 hour longer, until the meat is very tender.

3 Meanwhile, bring a medium saucepan of water to a boil. Add the bean sprouts and blanch for 30 seconds; drain. Put the cornstarch in a bowl and whisk in ½ cup of the liquid from the cooker.

4 With a slotted spoon, remove and discard the onions from the stew. Transfer the meat to a large bowl. Whisk the cornstarch mixture, then whisk it into the stew, cover and let simmer for 2 minutes. With 2 forks, very coarsely shred the meat. Return the meat to the cooker. Add the cabbage and pickles to the cooker, cover and cook until the cabbage is just wilted, 5 minutes. Turn the cooker off.

5 Spoon steamed rice into bowls. Ladle the stew over and around the rice. Top with the bean sprouts, a drizzle of sesame oil and the sliced scallions and serve.

Cheddar BLT Burgers *with* Russian Dressing

At BLT Burger in Las Vegas, chef Laurent Tourondel adds an unusual twist to a bacon cheeseburger: Russian dressing. His trick for perfect burgers is brushing the patties with butter while they're on the grill. The butter browns, making the meat exceptionally delicious.

A burger topped with both cheese and bacon requires a substantial red wine with strong, palate-cleansing tannins. Try a firm Cabernet from Washington State, such as the 2007 Ex-Libris or the 2007 Chateau Ste. Michelle Columbia Valley.

INGREDIENTS

½ cup mayonnaise

⅓ cup ketchup

1 tablespoon red wine vinegar

1 tablespoon grated onion

1 tablespoon chopped parsley

1 tablespoon chopped tarragon

1 teaspoon Worcestershire sauce

12 ounces thickly sliced bacon

1⅓ pounds ground beef chuck

1⅓ pounds ground beef sirloin

1 teaspoon kosher salt

½ teaspoon freshly ground pepper

2 tablespoons unsalted butter, melted

3 ounces sharp cheddar cheese, cut into 6 slices

6 hamburger buns, split and toasted

6 iceberg lettuce leaves

6 slices of tomato

6 slices of red onion

6 SERVINGS | TOTAL: 30 MIN

1 In a medium bowl, whisk the mayonnaise with the ketchup, red wine vinegar, onion, parsley, tarragon and Worcestershire sauce. Cover and refrigerate the Russian dressing.

2 In a large skillet, cook the bacon over moderately high heat, turning once, until crisp, about 6 minutes. Drain and cut the bacon into large pieces.

3 Light a grill and fill a large bowl with ice water. Gently mix the ground chuck with the ground sirloin, salt and pepper. Form the meat into six 4-inch patties about 1¼ inches thick. Submerge the patties in the cold water and let soak for 30 seconds. Immediately transfer the burgers to the grill and brush with some of the melted butter. Grill over high heat for 9 minutes for medium-rare meat, turning once or twice and brushing occasionally with butter. Top the burgers with the cheese during the last minute of grilling and let melt.

4 Spread the Russian dressing on the buns. Set the lettuce leaves and tomato slices on the bottom halves and top with the burgers, red onion and bacon. Close the burgers, cut in half and serve right away.

Chili *with* Hominy

To give his simple chili some flavor complexity, butcher Tom Mylan of the Meat Hook in Brooklyn, New York, uses three kinds of dried chiles: fruity guajillos, smoky anchos and a New Mexico chile. After he soaks the chiles in water to plump them, he blends them to form a puree to simmer with a mix of ground beef, pork and lamb.

Zinfandel's berry fruit and briary spice make it a natural partner for chili—it's an unpretentious wine for an unpretentious food. California, particularly Sonoma County, is the world's source for great Zinfandel. Look for the 2006 Teira Wines Sonoma County or the 2007 St. Francis Old Vines Sonoma County.

INGREDIENTS

- 8 guajillo chiles
- 2 ancho chiles
- 1 dried New Mexico chile
- 4 cups water
- 1½ tablespoons cumin seeds
- 2 tablespoons vegetable oil
- 2 large onions, coarsely chopped
- 8 garlic cloves, minced
- 2 pounds ground beef
- 1 pound ground pork
- ½ pound ground lamb
- One 28-ounce can hominy
- ¼ cup finely ground cornmeal
- Salt and freshly ground black pepper

8 SERVINGS | ACTIVE: 30 MIN; TOTAL: 2 HR 30 MIN

1 Break open the chiles and discard the stems and seeds. In a medium saucepan, cover the chiles with the water and bring to a boil. Cover the saucepan and remove from the heat. Let the chiles stand, stirring a few times, until very soft, about 1 hour. Working in batches, puree the chiles with their soaking liquid in a blender.

2 In a large pot, toast the cumin seeds over moderately high heat until fragrant, about 1 minute. Transfer the cumin seeds to a spice grinder and let cool completely. Grind the cumin seeds to a powder.

3 In the same pot, heat the oil. Add the onions and garlic and cook over moderately high heat, stirring occasionally, until softened, about 6 minutes. Add the ground beef, pork and lamb and cook, breaking up the meat into coarse chunks, until starting to brown, about 10 minutes. Add the ground cumin and cook, stirring, for 1 minute. Add the chile puree and simmer the chili over low heat for 1 hour, stirring occasionally.

4 Stir the hominy and its liquid into the chili. Gradually stir in the cornmeal. Simmer, stirring, until thickened, 5 minutes. Season the chili with salt and pepper and serve.

MAKE AHEAD The chili can be refrigerated for up to 3 days. Reheat gently before serving.

Supersize Meatballs *in* Marinara Sauce

To save time and create a dramatic-looking dish, food stylist Alison Attenborough and her chef husband, Jamie Kimm—authors of the award-winning book *Cooking for Friends*—supersize their meatballs. They use a mix of beef, pork and veal to lighten the texture and make the meatballs especially tasty.

For meatballs in a basic tomato sauce, a Sangiovese from Chianti Classico is a fail-safe pick, because its acidity matches the tanginess of the marinara. Try the 2007 Badia a Coltibuono or the 2008 Querciabella.

INGREDIENTS

¼ cup dry bread crumbs

¼ cup milk

1½ pounds mixed ground beef, pork and veal

½ small onion, minced

2 garlic cloves, minced

1 tablespoon chopped parsley

1 teaspoon minced oregano

1 egg, lightly beaten

1 tablespoon salt

¼ teaspoon freshly ground pepper

2 tablespoons extra-virgin olive oil

3½ cups marinara sauce

¾ pound spaghetti

Freshly shaved Parmigiano-Reggiano cheese, for serving

4 SERVINGS | TOTAL: 50 MIN

1 In a small bowl, combine the bread crumbs with the milk. In a large bowl, mix the ground meat with the soaked bread crumbs, the onion, garlic, parsley, oregano, egg, salt and pepper.

2 Form the meat mixture into 4 large balls. In a deep nonstick skillet, heat the olive oil. Add the meatballs and cook over moderately high heat, turning the meatballs occasionally, until browned all over, about 7 minutes. Add the marinara sauce to the skillet; cover and simmer over low heat for 30 minutes, until the meatballs are cooked through.

3 Meanwhile, in a large pot of boiling salted water, cook the spaghetti until al dente. Drain and serve with the meatballs, marinara and freshly shaved Parmigiano-Reggiano.

Middle Eastern Lamb Skewers

To update classic Middle Eastern kebabs, chef Michael Solomonov of Zahav in Philadelphia uses a surprising tenderizer: He adds onion juice or pureed onions to the marinade. The marinade is terrific on chicken breasts as well as lamb.

INGREDIENTS

1 medium onion, quartered

1 garlic clove, peeled

4 flat-leaf parsley sprigs

½ teaspoon finely grated lemon zest

3 tablespoons fresh lemon juice

1 teaspoon ground allspice

1 tablespoon kosher salt

Pinch of saffron threads

1¼ pounds trimmed lamb loin, cut into 1-inch cubes

2 tablespoons vegetable oil

Warm pita and plain Greek yogurt, for serving

4 SERVINGS | TOTAL: 30 MIN PLUS 6 HR MARINATING

1 In a blender, combine the onion, garlic, parsley sprigs, lemon zest, lemon juice, allspice, salt and saffron and puree until smooth. Transfer the marinade to a resealable plastic bag, add the cubed lamb and turn to coat. Seal the bag, pressing out any air. Refrigerate the lamb for at least 6 hours or preferably overnight.

2 Light a grill or preheat a grill pan. Drain the lamb, shaking off the excess marinade. Thread the lamb onto 4 long skewers, leaving a bit of room between the cubes. Brush the lamb with the oil and grill over high heat, turning occasionally, until lightly charred, about 5 minutes for medium-rare meat. Serve the lamb skewers with warm pita and Greek yogurt.

Subtly spicy Pinot Noirs, like those from California's Sonoma Coast, are a nice match with fragrant lamb skewers. Consider the 2007 Fogdog Pinot Noir from Freestone Vineyards or the 2007 Cep Vineyards Estate.

Basil-Crusted Leg of Lamb *with* Lemon Vinaigrette

Star chef Daniel Boulud does two ingenious things to a boneless, butterflied leg of lamb: He spreads a garlicky basil stuffing inside, then rolls up the meat, ties it up and sears it until nicely browned. Later, after the lamb is roasted, he tops it with more of the stuffing and broils it, creating a delicious crust.

Inky, herb-scented reds from Provence are spectacular with herb-crusted meats. Look for the 2008 Commanderie de Peyrassol La Croix or the 2006 Château de Pibarnon Bandol Rouge.

INGREDIENTS

- ¾ cup pine nuts (4 ounces)
- 2 cups packed basil leaves, plus 2 tablespoons chopped basil
- ⅔ cup plus 1 tablespoon extra-virgin olive oil—⅓ cup warmed
- 3 slices of packaged white bread, toasted and torn into pieces
- 2 garlic cloves, crushed
- 1 tablespoon finely grated lemon zest

- Kosher salt and freshly ground black pepper
- Cayenne pepper
- One 5-pound trimmed and butterflied boneless leg of lamb
- 3 tablespoons unsalted butter
- 2 thyme sprigs
- 3 tablespoons fresh lemon juice
- 1 teaspoon Dijon mustard

---

12 SERVINGS | ACTIVE: 45 MIN; TOTAL: 2 HR 30 MIN

1 Preheat the oven to 325°. Spread the pine nuts on a baking sheet and toast until golden, about 5 minutes. Let cool.

2 Fill a small bowl with ice water. In a small saucepan of boiling water, blanch the basil leaves for 10 seconds. Drain and immediately transfer to the ice water. Drain and squeeze dry. Place the basil in a food processor with the ⅓ cup of warmed oil and puree until fairly smooth. Add the toast, 1 of the garlic cloves, 2 teaspoons of the lemon zest and ½ cup of the pine nuts and pulse until coarsely chopped. Season with salt, black pepper and cayenne.

3 Set the lamb fat side down on a work surface and season it with salt and pepper. Rub half of the basil mixture on the meat. Roll up the meat and tie it at 1-inch intervals with kitchen string.

4 In a flameproof roasting pan, heat the 1 tablespoon of olive oil. Season the lamb with salt and pepper. Add the lamb to the roasting pan and cook over high heat, turning occasionally, until browned all over, 10 minutes. Add the butter, thyme and the remaining garlic clove to the roasting pan and cook for 1 minute, basting the lamb.

5 Transfer the lamb to the oven; roast for 1 hour and 15 minutes, turning once or twice, until an instant-read thermometer registers 130° for medium-rare meat. Transfer the lamb to a cutting board and remove the strings.

6 Preheat the broiler. Spread the remaining basil mixture over the roast and return the meat to the pan. Broil it 8 inches from the heat for 5 minutes, until the crust is lightly browned and sizzling. Transfer the meat to a cutting board; let rest for 20 minutes.

7 Meanwhile, in a bowl, whisk the lemon juice with the mustard. Whisk in the remaining ⅓ cup of oil, ¼ cup of pine nuts, 1 teaspoon of lemon zest and the chopped basil; season with salt and pepper. Slice the meat and transfer to plates. Drizzle with the vinaigrette and serve.

Grilled Lamb Chops *with* Roasted Garlic

Chef Robert Wiedmaier of Brabo restaurant and the Butcher's Block market in Alexandria, Virginia, serves his garlicky lamb chops with whole cloves of roasted garlic and a silky white bean puree in place of mashed potatoes. For added flavor, blend some of the roasted garlic into the bean puree as well.

 *Syrah is a classic match for lamb— its black-pepper notes taste great with gamey meats (it's good with goat, too). Southern France is Syrah's home, and there are still great bargains to be found, like the 2006 Layer Cake Côtes du Rhône Syrah and the 2006 Jean-Luc Colombo La Violette Syrah.*

INGREDIENTS

- ¼ cup extra-virgin olive oil, plus more for drizzling
- 4 thyme sprigs
- 1 garlic clove, minced, plus 2 heads of garlic, halved crosswise
- 2 teaspoons chopped rosemary
- ¼ teaspoon ground cumin
- 8 lamb loin chops
- 1 lemon, cut into ½-inch-thick slices (optional)
- Salt and freshly ground black pepper
- White Bean Puree (recipe follows), for serving

4 SERVINGS | ACTIVE: 20 MIN; TOTAL: 1 HR 30 MIN PLUS OVERNIGHT MARINATING

1 In a large, shallow dish, combine the ¼ cup of olive oil with the thyme, minced garlic, rosemary and cumin. Add the lamb chops and turn to coat with the marinade. Refrigerate overnight.

2 Preheat the oven to 350°. Set the halved heads of garlic cut side up on a baking sheet and drizzle with olive oil. Lay the lemon slices on another baking sheet and drizzle with olive oil. Cover both baking sheets with foil and roast for 1 hour, until the garlic is tender.

3 Light a grill. Remove the lamb chops from the marinade; discard the thyme and scrape off the garlic. Season the chops with salt and pepper and grill over moderate heat until lightly charred and medium-rare, 5 minutes per side. Serve the lamb chops with the roasted garlic and lemon slices and White Bean Puree.

White Bean Puree

- 3 tablespoons unsalted butter
- 1 small onion, finely diced
- 1 garlic clove, minced
- 1 thyme sprig
- Two 15-ounce cans cannellini beans, drained and rinsed
- 1 cup low-sodium chicken broth
- Salt and freshly ground pepper

4 SERVINGS | TOTAL: 25 MIN

In a medium saucepan, melt the butter. Add the onion, garlic and thyme sprig and cook over moderate heat, stirring a few times, until the onion is softened, about 7 minutes. Add the beans and broth and simmer over moderately high heat until the broth is reduced by half, about 5 minutes; discard the thyme sprig. Puree the bean mixture in a blender. Season the puree with salt and pepper and serve hot.
MAKE AHEAD The puree can be refrigerated for up to 3 days. Reheat gently.

Pan-Fried Pork Chops *with* Cranberry Relish

Recipe developer Rachel Soszynski updates the all-American dish of pan-fried pork chops with applesauce by swapping in a fresh, citrusy, spicy cranberry relish for the sweet apple puree.

These rich chops need a red wine with firm acidity, perhaps Barbera d'Alba, from Italy's Piedmont region. Consider the 2007 Bartolo Mascarello or the 2007 Conterno Fantino Vignota.

INGREDIENTS

- 2 cups frozen cranberries (8 ounces), thawed
- 1 serrano chile, seeded and chopped
- ½ cup sugar
- ⅓ cup fresh orange juice
- 1 tablespoon finely grated orange zest

- Salt
- 2 tablespoons olive oil
- Four 5-ounce bone-in pork loin chops
- Freshly ground pepper
- ½ cup chopped cilantro

4 SERVINGS | ☉ | TOTAL: 40 MIN

1 In a food processor, puree the cranberries with the serrano chile, sugar, orange juice, orange zest and 1 teaspoon of salt.

2 In a large skillet, heat the olive oil until shimmering. Season the pork chops with salt and pepper, add them to the skillet and cook over moderately high heat until they are browned and cooked through, about 4 minutes per side. Transfer the pork chops to a plate and let them stand for 5 minutes.

3 Add the cranberry relish to the skillet and cook, scraping up any browned bits from the bottom of the pan, until hot, about 2 minutes. Add any pork juices to the relish and stir in the cilantro. Transfer the pork chops to plates and serve with the cranberry relish.

SERVE WITH Sautéed green beans.

Citrus-Marinated Pork Rib Roast

To create an incredibly aromatic marinade for this elegant roast, chef Fabio Trabocchi adds a double dose of citrus (lemon and orange) to a traditional mix of herbs: rosemary, fennel, juniper berries and bay leaves. He uses a standing rib roast because the top layer of fat melts and bastes the pork as it roasts, making the meat extra juicy.

The area around Montalcino in Tuscany produces aromatic, graceful reds; among them is Brunello di Montalcino, one of Italy's greatest wines, which can age effortlessly for years. Brunello is an ideal partner for almost any extravagant roast. Chef Trabocchi likes the 2004 Tenuta Il Poggione; another great choice is the 2004 Antinori Pian delle Vigne.

INGREDIENTS

Two 5-bone pork rib roasts (about 4 pounds each)

6 garlic cloves

6 whole cloves

3 lemons, zest removed in strips with a vegetable peeler and lemons juiced

3 oranges, zest removed in strips with a vegetable peeler and oranges juiced

20 fresh bay leaves

8 rosemary sprigs

2 tablespoons fennel seeds, coarsely chopped

1 tablespoon juniper berries, coarsely chopped

½ cup extra-virgin olive oil

Salt and freshly ground pepper

Roasted small apples and pears (see Note), for garnish

10 SERVINGS | ACTIVE: 45 MIN;
TOTAL: 2 HR 30 MIN PLUS OVERNIGHT MARINATING

1 Using a paring knife, make three 1-inch-deep slits on the fatty side of each pork rib roast closest to the bones. Stud the garlic cloves with the whole cloves and stuff them into the slits.

2 In a baking dish, combine the lemon and orange zests and juices with the bay leaves, rosemary sprigs, fennel seeds, juniper berries and ¼ cup of the olive oil. Add the pork and turn to coat. Cover and refrigerate overnight, turning occasionally. Bring the pork rib roasts to room temperature before roasting.

3 Preheat the oven to 350°. Scrape off the marinade and generously season the pork with salt and pepper. In a very large skillet, heat the remaining ¼ cup of olive oil. Add the pork and brown over moderate heat, turning occasionally, about 15 minutes.

4 Transfer the pork rib roasts to a large roasting pan. Roast for about 1 hour and 20 minutes, rotating the pan once or twice, until an instant-read thermometer inserted into the thickest part of the meat registers 140°. Transfer the pork to a cutting board and let rest for 20 minutes. Cut the pork between the rib bones into 10 chops. Transfer to plates, garnish with the roasted apples and pears and serve.
NOTE Score the apples to prevent the skin from splitting. Roast the fruit at 350° for about 1 hour, until tender.

Spicy & Sticky Baby Back Ribs

Five years ago, smoked paprika wasn't part of the American food lexicon. New Orleans chef Donald Link of Cochon uses the spice—along with cayenne, black pepper and hot sauce—to update barbecued ribs. His cooking method is also smart: Slow-roasting the ribs at a low temperature makes them sticky; broiling at the end makes the edges crispy.

Shiraz from Australia's Barossa region sometimes has a bad rep for being too jammy and concentrated, but these over-the-top wines are the perfect pairing for these intense ribs. Look for the 2008 Strong Arms or the 2008 Hewitson Ned & Henry's Barossa Valley.

INGREDIENTS

- 1 cup dark brown sugar
- 3 tablespoons kosher salt
- 1 tablespoon dry mustard
- 1 tablespoon ground fennel
- 1 tablespoon freshly ground black pepper
- 1 tablespoon cayenne pepper
- 1 tablespoon sweet smoked paprika
- 4 racks baby back ribs (about 2½ pounds each), membrane removed from the underside of each rack

- 1 tablespoon unsalted butter
- 1 small onion, minced
- 3 garlic cloves, minced
- 1½ teaspoons dried thyme
- 1 cup ketchup
- 1 cup cider vinegar
- 1 cup beef broth
- ¼ cup hot sauce
- ¼ cup Worcestershire sauce
- 2 tablespoons unsulfured molasses

6 TO 8 SERVINGS
ACTIVE: 40 MIN; TOTAL: 4 HR PLUS OVERNIGHT SEASONING

1 In a small bowl, combine the brown sugar, salt, mustard, fennel, black pepper, cayenne and paprika. On 2 large rimmed baking sheets, sprinkle the spice mix all over the ribs, pressing and patting it. Cover with aluminum foil and refrigerate overnight.

2 Preheat the oven to 250°. Pour off any liquid on the baking sheets, cover the ribs with aluminum foil and roast for about 3 hours, until the meat is tender but not falling off the bone. Pour off any liquid on the baking sheets.

3 Meanwhile, in a saucepan, melt the butter. Add the onion, garlic and thyme and cook over moderate heat until the onion is softened, about 5 minutes. Add the ketchup, vinegar, beef broth, hot sauce, Worcestershire sauce and molasses and bring to a boil. Simmer over low heat, stirring occasionally, until thickened, about 30 minutes.

4 Preheat the broiler and position a rack 10 inches from the heat. Brush the ribs liberally with the barbecue sauce and broil for about 10 minutes, turning and brushing occasionally with the sauce, until well-browned and crispy in spots. Transfer the ribs to a work surface and let rest for 5 minutes. Cut in between the bones and mound the ribs on a platter. Pass any extra barbecue sauce on the side.

MAKE AHEAD The roasted ribs and the barbecue sauce can be refrigerated separately for up to 4 days. Return them both to room temperature and broil the ribs just before serving.

Thai Ground Pork Salad

The Thai salad known as *larb* or *laab* is a wonderfully tasty combination of ground pork spiked with chiles, lime juice and fish sauce served with shredded cabbage. In his version, butcher Tom Mylan of the Meat Hook in Brooklyn, New York, uses readily available jalapeños in place of Thai chiles and serves the salad with whole Boston lettuce leaves for wrapping.

INGREDIENTS

- 2 pounds ground pork
- 2 garlic cloves, minced
- 2 small shallots, minced
- 1 large jalapeño, seeded and minced, plus sliced jalapeño for garnish

Juice of 1 lime, plus lime wedges for serving

- 2 tablespoons Asian fish sauce
- 1 teaspoon light brown sugar
- 1 teaspoon Sriracha chile sauce, plus more for serving
- 1 tablespoon vegetable oil
- ½ cup chopped cilantro
- ½ cup chopped mint
- ½ cup chopped basil

Salt and freshly ground pepper

- 1 cup chopped salted peanuts
- 1 large head of Boston or other leafy lettuce, separated

6 SERVINGS | 🙂 | TOTAL: 40 MIN

1 In a large bowl, mix the pork, garlic, shallots and minced jalapeño. In a small bowl, whisk the lime juice, fish sauce, brown sugar and the 1 teaspoon of Sriracha.

2 In a large skillet, heat the vegetable oil. Add the pork mixture and cook over high heat, stirring to break up the meat, until no pink remains, 5 minutes. Remove from the heat and stir in the lime juice mixture. Let stand for 5 minutes. Transfer the meat to a bowl, then stir in the herbs and season with salt and pepper. Top with the peanuts and sliced jalapeños. Serve with lime wedges, Sriracha and lettuce for wrapping.

Though most spicy Thai dishes go well with slightly sweet white wines, this hearty pork dish would match best with a red wine that has enough fruit to cool the heat a bit. Reds from Austria, such as Zweigelt and Blaufränkisch, would be delicious here. Try the 2007 Nittnaus Blauer Zweigelt or the 2006 Weninger Hochäcker Blaufränkisch.

Roasted Veal Chops *with* Grapes

Roast rack of veal with a reduced-wine sauce is one of the fanciest classics a home cook can make. Cookbook author Melissa Clark turns it into a superfast one-dish meal. First, instead of dealing with a rack of veal, she buys individual chops and roasts them on a single baking sheet. Second, she tosses grapes with sherry vinegar and butter and roasts them alongside the chops to mix with the pan juices for a sauce.

Light-bodied Beaujolais made with the Gamay grape is low in tannins, making it an excellent partner for lighter meat dishes like these chops. The 2008 Jean-Paul Thévenet Vieilles Vignes Morgon and the 2007 Louis Claude Desvignes Javernières Morgon are both terrific.

INGREDIENTS

- 1 pound seedless red grapes
- 3 tablespoons sherry vinegar
- 2½ tablespoons unsalted butter, softened
- ½ teaspoon sugar
- Salt and freshly ground pepper
- Four 1-inch-thick veal rib chops (about ½ pound each)

4 SERVINGS | TOTAL: 25 MIN

1 Preheat the oven to 500°. On a sturdy rimmed baking sheet, toss the grapes with the vinegar, 1½ tablespoons of the softened butter and the sugar; season with salt and pepper. Roast for about 10 minutes, shaking the baking sheet halfway through, until the grapes are hot and the pan is sizzling.

2 Rub the veal chops with the remaining 1 tablespoon of butter and season with salt and pepper. Push the grapes to one side of the baking sheet. Add the veal chops and roast for about 5 minutes, or until sizzling underneath. Turn the chops and roast for 5 minutes longer for medium-rare meat. Transfer the veal chops to a platter, scrape the grapes and juices on top and serve.

Italian-Sausage Burgers *with* Garlicky Spinach

Italian sausage is the secret—and only—ingredient in these fast and flavorful burgers from FOOD & WINE's Grace Parisi. Because the sausage meat is already seasoned, all she does is remove it from the casings, form it into patties and grill it. Anchovy paste adds a fast hit of flavor to the garlicky sautéed spinach topping.

INGREDIENTS

10 ounces baby spinach
2 tablespoons extra-virgin olive oil, plus more for brushing
2 garlic cloves, minced
1 teaspoon anchovy paste (optional)
Salt

1 pound sweet or hot Italian sausages (or a combination of both), casings removed
4 slices of provolone cheese
¼ cup sun-dried-tomato pesto
4 round ciabatta rolls, split and toasted

4 SERVINGS | TOTAL: 30 MIN

1 In a large skillet, bring ¼ inch of water to a boil. Add the spinach and cook, stirring, until just wilted, about 1 minute; drain and press out as much water as possible. Wipe out the skillet.

2 In the same skillet, heat the 2 tablespoons of olive oil until shimmering. Add the garlic and anchovy paste and cook over high heat, stirring, until fragrant, 1 minute. Add the spinach, season with salt and stir just until coated, about 10 seconds.

3 Light a grill or preheat a grill pan. Using slightly moistened hands, form the sausage meat into four 4-inch patties about ¾ inch thick. Brush the burgers with oil and grill over moderate heat until browned and crusty on the bottom, about 5 minutes. Carefully flip the burgers. Top with the cheese and grill until the burgers are cooked through and the cheese is melted, about 5 minutes longer. Spread the pesto on the rolls, top with the burgers and spinach and serve.

Italian sausage needs a robust red wine like Zinfandel. Coincidentally, superstar Zinfandel producer Peter Seghesio and his family make their own Italian sausage every year to give as holiday gifts. Look for his basic 2008 Seghesio Sonoma Zinfandel or the single-vineyard 2008 Seghesio Home Ranch bottling.

Salads & Vegetables

Watermelon Salad *with* Feta

Cookbook author Melissa Clark adds two new ingredients to the traditional Greek pairing of watermelon and feta: oil-cured olives to make the mixture more complex, and the Tunisian chile paste harissa to give it a spicy kick.

INGREDIENTS

¼ cup extra-virgin olive oil

1½ tablespoons fresh lemon juice

½ teaspoon harissa or other hot sauce

Salt and freshly ground pepper

1½ pounds seedless watermelon, rind removed and fruit sliced ¼ inch thick

½ small red onion, thinly sliced

¼ cup coarsely chopped flat-leaf parsley

¼ cup pitted oil-cured black olives, preferably Moroccan, coarsely chopped

½ cup crumbled feta cheese

4 SERVINGS | TOTAL: 20 MIN

In a small bowl, whisk the olive oil with the lemon juice and harissa and season the dressing with salt and pepper. Arrange the watermelon slices in a serving bowl and sprinkle with the sliced red onion, chopped parsley and olives and crumbled feta. Drizzle the dressing on top of the watermelon salad and serve.

Caesar Salad *with* Crispy Tofu Croutons

In this creative remix of a classic Caesar, FOOD & WINE's Melissa Rubel Jacobson pan-fries tofu cubes until they become crisp and crouton-like. She also blends soft tofu with olive oil, lemon juice and an anchovy to make a terrific Caesar-style dressing without the standard raw egg yolks.

✳ *For an excellent green-salad wine, look for zippy, fruity Vermentino, a white from the mountainous Italian island of Sardinia. Two great examples: the 2008 Cantina Santa Maria La Palma Aragosta and the 2008 Sella & Mosca La Cala.*

INGREDIENTS

- 6 ounces soft silken tofu, drained
- 1½ tablespoons extra-virgin olive oil
- 1½ tablespoons fresh lemon juice
- 1½ tablespoons freshly grated Parmigiano-Reggiano cheese, plus freshly shaved Parmigiano for serving
- 1 oil-packed anchovy fillet, drained
- 1 small garlic clove
- ½ teaspoon Worcestershire sauce
- ½ teaspoon Dijon mustard
- Salt and freshly ground pepper
- One 14-ounce package firm tofu, drained and cut into ¾-inch cubes
- Vegetable oil, for frying
- ½ cup cornstarch
- 2 romaine hearts (1 pound), torn into bite-size pieces

4 SERVINGS | ⏲ | TOTAL: 30 MIN

1 In a blender, puree the silken tofu with the olive oil, lemon juice, the 1½ tablespoons of Parmigiano, the anchovy, garlic, Worcestershire and mustard; season the dressing with salt and pepper.

2 Wrap the firm tofu in paper towels and press out some of the water. In a large skillet, heat ¼ inch of vegetable oil until shimmering. In a bowl, toss the tofu with the cornstarch until coated. Add the cubes to the oil and fry over moderately high heat, turning once, until crisp, about 8 minutes. Using a slotted spoon, transfer the croutons to a paper towel–lined plate; season with salt.

3 In a large bowl, toss the romaine with the dressing and two-thirds of the croutons. Transfer the salad to plates, top with the remaining croutons and freshly shaved Parmigiano and serve.

Grilled Tuna Niçoise Salad

FOOD & WINE's Melissa Rubel Jacobson deconstructs the traditional *salade niçoise*, replacing oil-packed tuna with lighter grilled tuna steaks. She turns the other ingredients into two composed salads: green beans and cherry tomatoes, and fingerling potato coins—all tossed in one tangy fresh-herb dressing.

✳ *Provence is the birthplace of both Niçoise salad and bright, refreshing rosé. The 2009 Domaine Houchart Côtes de Provence and the 2008 l'Estandon Côtes de Provence are natural pairings for the salad.*

INGREDIENTS

TUNA
- ½ cup extra-virgin olive oil
- ½ cup dry white wine
- 2½ tablespoons Dijon mustard
- 1 tablespoon coarsely chopped thyme
- 1 tablespoon plus 1 teaspoon ground fennel
- 2 large shallots, coarsely chopped
- Ten 1-inch-thick tuna steaks (8 ounces each)
- Kosher salt and freshly ground pepper

SALAD
- 2 pounds green beans
- 3 pounds fingerling potatoes
- 1 tablespoon Dijon mustard
- 4 tablespoons red wine vinegar
- ½ cup plus 2 tablespoons extra-virgin olive oil
- Kosher salt and freshly ground pepper
- 2 tablespoons chopped parsley
- 1 tablespoon chopped tarragon
- 1 tablespoon snipped chives
- ½ teaspoon chopped thyme
- ½ pound cherry tomatoes, halved

10 MAIN-COURSE SERVINGS | ACTIVE: 35 MIN; TOTAL: 1 HR

1 ***Marinate the tuna*** In a medium bowl, whisk the olive oil with the wine, mustard, thyme, fennel and shallots. Arrange the tuna steaks on a large rimmed baking sheet and pour the marinade over them. Turn the tuna steaks to coat. Let stand for 30 minutes.

2 ***Meanwhile, make the salad*** Bring a large pot of salted water to a boil. Add the green beans and cook until crisp-tender, about 5 minutes. Using a slotted spoon, remove the beans, transfer to a baking sheet and pat dry. Return the water to a boil, add the potatoes and cook until just tender, 8 to 10 minutes. Drain, let cool and cut the potatoes into ½-inch slices.

3 In a large bowl, whisk the mustard with the vinegar. Gradually whisk in the olive oil and season with salt and pepper. Whisk in the parsley, tarragon, chives and thyme.

4 In a bowl, toss the green beans with half of the vinaigrette. Add the tomatoes and toss gently. In another bowl, toss the potatoes with the remaining vinaigrette.

5 ***Grill the tuna*** Light a grill or preheat a grill pan. Season the tuna steaks with salt and pepper. Grill over moderately high heat, turning once, for 4 minutes per side, until medium. Thinly slice the tuna steaks, transfer them to plates and serve with the green beans, tomatoes and potatoes.

SERVE WITH Hard-boiled eggs, Niçoise olives and marinated anchovies.

Arugula Salad *with* Shiitake Mushrooms

Cooks in Italy often match peppery arugula with sweet ingredients like oranges or creamy ones like goat cheese. Taking inspiration from Asia, FOOD & WINE's Marcia Kiesel emphasizes the green's spiciness by tossing it with mild sautéed shiitake and fresh mint.

INGREDIENTS

2 tablespoons mayonnaise

1 teaspoon finely grated lemon zest

1½ teaspoons fresh lemon juice

3 tablespoons extra-virgin olive oil

Salt and freshly ground pepper

1 tablespoon vegetable oil

½ pound shiitake mushrooms, stems discarded and caps thinly sliced

½ pound arugula, thick stems discarded

⅓ cup thinly sliced mint

4 SERVINGS | TOTAL: 35 MIN

1 In a small bowl, whisk the mayonnaise with the grated lemon zest and the lemon juice, then whisk in the olive oil until smooth. Season the dressing with salt and pepper.

2 In a large skillet, heat the vegetable oil. Add the sliced shiitake and season with salt and pepper. Cover and cook over moderate heat, stirring a few times, until tender and browned, about 8 minutes. Transfer to a plate and let cool to room temperature.

3 In a large bowl, toss the arugula with the mushrooms and mint. Pour the dressing over the salad, toss well and serve.

Sweet Corn Succotash

Succotash—an inexpensive staple of the Great Depression—is a simple mixture of corn and beans, usually lima. In his updated succotash, chef Chris Hastings of Hot and Hot Fish Club in Birmingham, Alabama, uses fresh field peas, like black-eyed peas, or nicely sweet green peas. Then he makes the mixture a bit fancier by adding bacon, onion, basil and tomatoes.

INGREDIENTS

2 cups fresh green peas

1 tablespoon canola oil

1 thick slice of bacon, finely diced

1 small onion, finely chopped

½ pound okra, sliced ½ inch thick

3 medium tomatoes—peeled, seeded and coarsely chopped

3 ears of corn, kernels cut off

Salt and freshly ground pepper

2 tablespoons unsalted butter

¼ cup slivered basil

4 SERVINGS | ⏱ | TOTAL: 45 MIN

1 In a large pot of boiling salted water, cook the peas until tender, about 5 minutes. Drain, reserving ¾ cup of the cooking liquid.

2 In a deep skillet, heat the oil. Add the bacon and cook over moderately high heat until browned, about 5 minutes. Add the onion and cook until just softened, about 5 minutes longer. Add the okra and cook for 8 minutes. Add the tomatoes and corn and cook, stirring occasionally, until the tomatoes break down, 10 to 12 minutes. Add the peas with the reserved cooking liquid, season with salt and pepper and simmer the succotash for 2 minutes. Stir in the butter and slivered basil, then serve.

Broccolini *with* Crispy Lemon Crumbs

Instead of using broccoli for this recipe, *Top Chef* judge and FOOD & WINE special-projects director Gail Simmons opts for Broccolini, a fairly new cross between broccoli and *gai lan* (Chinese kale). The tiny broccoli-like florets are sweet and the tender stem has a subtle peppery edge—both excellent with the lemony bread crumb topping.

INGREDIENTS

- 2 slices of white bread, torn
- 2 tablespoons unsalted butter
- ½ teaspoon crushed red pepper
- 1 teaspoon finely grated lemon zest

Salt

- 2 bunches of Broccolini (8 ounces each), ends trimmed
- 3 tablespoons extra-virgin olive oil
- 1 small shallot, very finely chopped

Lemon wedges, for serving

6 SERVINGS | TOTAL: 30 MIN

1 In a food processor, pulse the white bread until large crumbs form. In a large skillet, melt the butter. Add the bread crumbs and cook over moderate heat, stirring constantly, until golden. Remove from the heat. Stir in the crushed red pepper and lemon zest and season with salt. Transfer the crumbs to a plate to cool. Wipe out the skillet.

2 Bring a large pot of salted water to a boil. Add the Broccolini and cook until crisp-tender, about 3 minutes. Drain well, shaking off the excess water; pat dry.

3 In the large skillet, heat the olive oil until shimmering. Add the shallot and cook over moderate heat, stirring, until lightly browned, about 1 minute. Add the Broccolini, season lightly with salt and cook, stirring occasionally, until lightly browned in spots, about 4 minutes. Transfer the Broccolini to a serving platter and sprinkle the lemony bread crumbs on top. Serve right away, with lemon wedges.

MAKE AHEAD The lemon crumbs can be stored in an airtight container at room temperature for up to 2 days.

Roasted Cauliflower *with* Green Olives & Pine Nuts

In the amount of time it takes to roast cauliflower by itself, FOOD & WINE's Grace Parisi adds a few key ingredients to make a terrific side dish: After roasting the florets for 20 minutes, she tosses them with pine nuts, parsley, olives and capers and cooks them for 10 minutes more. The resulting mix of Mediterranean flavors and sweet, caramelized cauliflower is great with roast chicken or steamed fish.

INGREDIENTS

- 1 pound cauliflower, cut into 1-inch florets
- 2 tablespoons extra-virgin olive oil

Salt and freshly ground pepper

- 2 tablespoons pine nuts
- ⅓ cup sliced pitted green olives
- 1 tablespoon chopped flat-leaf parsley
- 1 tablespoon drained capers

4 SERVINGS | ⏱ | ACTIVE: 10 MIN; TOTAL: 40 MIN

Preheat the oven to 425°. In a shallow 1½-quart baking dish, toss the cauliflower florets with the olive oil and season with salt and pepper. Roast for 20 minutes, or until the cauliflower is lightly browned in spots. Add the pine nuts, olives, parsley and capers, toss and roast for about 10 minutes longer, until the pine nuts are lightly toasted. Serve the cauliflower warm or at room temperature.

Sautéed Sesame Green Beans

Sautéed green beans are a versatile side dish. FOOD & WINE's Melissa Rubel Jacobson gives them some personality in this Asian-inspired recipe by sautéing the beans in peanut oil, then tossing them with toasted sesame oil and sesame seeds. For a Mediterranean version, use olive oil and lemon zest; for an Indian one, peanut oil and toasted cumin and mustard seeds.

INGREDIENTS

- 1 pound green beans, trimmed
- 1 tablespoon peanut oil
- 1 tablespoon toasted sesame seeds
- 1½ teaspoons toasted sesame oil
- Kosher salt and freshly ground pepper

4 TO 6 SERVINGS | TOTAL: 20 MIN

1 Fill a medium bowl with ice water. Fill a large skillet with ¼ inch of salted water and bring to a boil. Add the green beans, cover and steam until crisp-tender, about 4 minutes. Drain and transfer the green beans to the ice water until chilled, about 3 minutes. Drain again and pat dry.

2 When ready to serve, wipe out the skillet and heat the peanut oil until shimmering. Add the green beans and cook over moderate heat, tossing occasionally, until heated through, about 3 minutes. Add the sesame seeds and sesame oil, then season with salt and pepper. Transfer the green beans to plates and serve.

Fresh Vegetable Curry

Indian curries can include a dozen or more spices, plus serrano or bird chiles for heat. For this simplified curry, chef Vikram Sunderam of Rasika in Washington, DC, opts for readily available jalapeño pepper instead of the more exotic chiles and pares down the spices to just turmeric (lauded for its healthful anti-inflammatory properties). Augmented with garlic and ginger, the sweet, spicy sauce is fantastic over rice.

✻ *Dishes with lots of spice and many different kinds of vegetables can be challenging to pair with wine. So match this vegetable curry with a beer like Dale's Pale Ale (it comes in a can) or Tröegs Pale Ale from Pennsylvania.*

INGREDIENTS

- 2 tablespoons canola oil
- 1 small onion, thinly sliced
- 2 tablespoons finely julienned fresh ginger (from a 2-inch piece)
- 1 jalapeño, seeded and cut into thin strips
- 2 bay leaves
- 3 garlic cloves, minced
- 1 teaspoon turmeric
- 2 small tomatoes, coarsely chopped

- One 14-ounce can unsweetened coconut milk
- ¼ cup water
- Kosher salt
- 3 carrots, quartered lengthwise and cut into 1-inch pieces
- 1 pound butternut squash (neck only), peeled and cut into 1-by-½-inch pieces (1½ cups)
- ½ pound thin green beans, cut into 1-inch pieces
- Basmati rice, for serving

---

4 TO 6 SERVINGS | ACTIVE: 20 MIN; TOTAL: 1 HR

1 In a large, deep skillet, heat the oil. Add the onion, ginger, jalapeño and bay leaves and cook over moderate heat until the vegetables are softened, about 5 minutes. Add the garlic and turmeric and cook, stirring, for 2 minutes. Add the tomatoes and mash lightly until just beginning to soften, 2 minutes. Add the coconut milk and water, season with salt and bring to a boil.

2 Add the carrots, cover and simmer over low heat until crisp-tender, about 12 minutes. Add the squash and beans, cover and simmer until tender, 15 minutes. Remove and discard the bay leaves. Serve the curry with basmati rice.

MAKE AHEAD The curry can be refrigerated overnight.

Layered Eggplant, Zucchini & Tomato Casserole

This is a lightened take on the countless zucchini-tomato-eggplant casseroles created by home cooks to use up summer produce. Instead of layering cheese and bread crumbs with raw vegetables, FOOD & WINE's Marcia Kiesel roasts the zucchini and eggplant first, concentrating their flavors. Then she layers the roasted vegetables with sautéed tomatoes, feta and bread crumbs. Baking the casserole creates an irresistible crust on top.

The Mediterranean ingredients in this dish, from the eggplant to the basil to the feta, immediately suggest a sunny Provençal rosé. Look for the pricey but elegant 2009 Domaine Tempier Bandol or the less-expensive 2009 Commanderie de la Bargemone.

INGREDIENTS

- 3 tablespoons extra-virgin olive oil, plus more for greasing and brushing
- 3 medium zucchini (1½ pounds), sliced lengthwise ¼ inch thick
- 2 long, narrow eggplants (1½ pounds), peeled and sliced lengthwise ⅓ inch thick

Salt and freshly ground pepper

- 1 large shallot, minced
- 1 pound plum tomatoes, cut into ½-inch dice
- 3 ounces feta cheese, crumbled (¾ cup)
- ¼ cup chopped basil
- ⅓ cup *panko* or coarse dry bread crumbs

6 SERVINGS | ACTIVE: 30 MIN; TOTAL: 1 HR

1 Preheat the oven to 425°. Oil 2 large rimmed baking sheets. Put the zucchini slices on one sheet and the eggplant on the other. Brush the slices all over with oil and season with salt and pepper. Arrange the slices on each sheet in a slightly overlapping layer. Bake for 15 minutes, until the vegetables are tender.

2 Meanwhile, in a large skillet, heat 2 tablespoons of the oil. Add the shallot and cook over moderate heat until softened, 3 minutes. Add the tomatoes and cook over high heat until slightly softened and bubbling, 1 minute. Season with salt and pepper.

3 Oil a large, shallow baking dish (about 15 by 10 inches). Lay half of the eggplant in the dish and spread one-fourth of the tomatoes on top. Scatter with half of the feta and basil. Layer half of the zucchini on top, followed by another one-fourth of the tomatoes and the remaining basil, eggplant and zucchini. Top with the remaining tomatoes and feta. Mix the *panko* with the remaining 1 tablespoon of oil and sprinkle over the casserole. Bake in the upper third of the oven for 20 minutes, until bubbling and crisp. Let stand for 5 minutes, then serve hot or warm.

Cheese-Stuffed Grilled Peppers

Robert Perkins and John Lancaster, wine directors at San Francisco's Boulevard restaurant, love making this grilled version of classic batter-fried chiles rellenos. They use an assortment of medium-size peppers: mild green Anaheims, spicier Cubanelles, rich poblanos, baby bells. As the peppers blister, the mixture of ricotta, Parmesan and cream cheese tucked inside turns warm and gooey.

INGREDIENTS

1 cup ricotta cheese (8 ounces)

1 cup cream cheese (8 ounces), at room temperature

½ cup freshly grated Parmigiano-Reggiano cheese

Salt and freshly ground pepper

4 Anaheim or Cubanelle peppers (see Note)

4 baby bell peppers

4 small poblano chiles

Extra-virgin olive oil, for rubbing

4 SERVINGS | ☺ | TOTAL: 30 MIN

1 In a medium bowl, blend the ricotta cheese with the cream cheese and Parmigiano-Reggiano. Season with salt and pepper.

2 Light a grill or heat a grill pan. Using a small, sharp knife, remove the stems from the peppers and reserve. Cut around inside the peppers to detach the membranes and remove the seeds. Using a butter knife, fill the peppers with the cheese mixture and reattach the tops. Rub the peppers with olive oil.

3 Grill the stuffed peppers over moderately high heat, turning occasionally, until the peppers are blistered all over and the cheese filling is piping hot, about 7 minutes. Transfer the grilled stuffed peppers to plates and serve.

MAKE AHEAD The cheese-filled peppers can be refrigerated overnight. Bring to room temperature before grilling.

Wines with a touch of sweetness, such as Pinot Blanc, pair well with piquant peppers. The 2008 Skylark Orsi Vineyard Pinot Blanc is from California's Mendocino region; the 2009 Alois Lageder Pinot Bianco is a crisp Italian take on the same grape variety.

Potato Salad *with* Hummus-Yogurt Dressing

In this clever potato salad remake, FOOD & WINE's Grace Parisi uses yogurt and hummus to make one great and very speedy dressing.

INGREDIENTS

- 2 pounds Yukon Gold potatoes, scrubbed
- ½ cup hummus
- ¾ cup nonfat plain yogurt
- 1 cup finely diced celery
- ¼ cup finely diced cornichons
- ¼ cup chopped flat-leaf parsley
- 3 tablespoons finely diced red onion

Salt and freshly ground pepper

6 SERVINGS | ☉ | ACTIVE: 20 MIN; TOTAL: 45 MIN

1 In a large pot, cover the potatoes with water and bring to a boil. Simmer over moderate heat until the potatoes are tender when pierced with a knife, about 20 minutes. Drain and let cool. Peel the potatoes and cut into 1-inch pieces.

2 In a large bowl, mix the hummus with the yogurt, celery, cornichons, parsley and onion. Fold in the potatoes, season with salt and pepper and serve at once.

MAKE AHEAD The potato salad can be refrigerated overnight.

Mashed Potatoes *with* Crispy Shallots

Although russets are the traditional choice for mashed potatoes, Yukon Golds have a naturally creamy texture that arguably makes them a better option. For ultrafluffy mashed potatoes, FOOD & WINE's Grace Parisi presses the cooked potatoes through a ricer. (A food mill or a fine-mesh sieve works, too, but if you choose to mash by hand, be gentle or the potatoes will turn gluey.) The fried-shallot topping adds a fantastic oniony crunch.

INGREDIENTS

6 pounds Yukon Gold potatoes, peeled and quartered

4 garlic cloves, peeled

2 cups canola oil

6 large shallots, thinly sliced (1½ cups)

1 cup half-and-half

1½ sticks (6 ounces) unsalted butter

Kosher salt

12 SERVINGS | ⏱ | TOTAL: 45 MIN

1 In a large pot, cover the potatoes and garlic cloves with cold water and bring to a boil. Simmer over moderate heat until the potatoes are tender when pierced with a fork, about 20 minutes.

2 Meanwhile, in a medium skillet, heat the oil until shimmering. Add the shallots in a single layer and cook over moderate heat, stirring frequently, until golden, about 15 minutes. Using a slotted spoon, transfer the shallots to paper towels to drain.

3 Drain the potatoes and garlic in a colander, shaking out the excess water. Add the half-and-half and butter to the pot and heat until melted. Remove from the heat. Press the potatoes and garlic through a ricer into the pot and season with salt. Stir and cook over moderate heat until very hot. Transfer the mashed potatoes to a bowl. Just before serving, sprinkle the shallots with salt and garnish the mashed potatoes with the crispy shallots.

MAKE AHEAD The mashed potatoes can be made earlier in the day and kept at room temperature; warm over moderate heat, stirring constantly. The fried shallots can be kept in an airtight container for up to 3 days; reheat in the oven if desired.

Sweet Potato Casserole

Southern cooks often top sweet potato casserole with a mixture of brown sugar, butter and pecans. Alabama-born sculptor and home cook Sandi Stevens McGee covers her silky pureed sweet potatoes with an especially crunchy pecan-cornflake topping. If she doesn't have pecans or cornflakes on hand, she'll make the topping with whatever nuts and cereal are in her cupboard.

INGREDIENTS

5½ pounds sweet potatoes, peeled and cut into 2-inch chunks

2 sticks (8 ounces) unsalted butter, melted, plus more for brushing

Salt

1½ teaspoons freshly grated nutmeg

1½ cups light brown sugar

1 cup milk, warmed

3 large eggs, beaten

1 cup pecan halves (4 ounces)

1 cup cornflakes

½ teaspoon cinnamon

12 SERVINGS | ACTIVE: 45 MIN; TOTAL: 2 HR 30 MIN

1 Preheat the oven to 350°. Butter a 13-by-9-inch baking dish. Put the sweet potatoes in a large pot. Cover with cold water and bring to a boil. Cook over moderate heat until the sweet potatoes are tender, about 15 minutes. Drain well, shaking off the excess water. Transfer the sweet potatoes to a food processor (in batches, if necessary) and puree until smooth.

2 Scrape the puree into a large bowl. Add half of the melted butter, 2 teaspoons of salt, 1 teaspoon of the nutmeg, ½ cup of the brown sugar and the milk and stir until combined. Stir in the eggs. Pour the mixture into the prepared baking dish and smooth the surface. Cover with foil and bake for 40 minutes.

3 Meanwhile, spread the pecans on a baking sheet and bake for 5 minutes, until lightly toasted. Transfer the pecans to a work surface and coarsely chop them. In a bowl, toss the pecans with the cornflakes, cinnamon and the remaining melted butter, ½ teaspoon of nutmeg and 1 cup of brown sugar. Season the topping with salt.

4 Remove the foil from the casserole. Spoon small clumps of the topping all over the sweet potatoes. Bake, uncovered, for 40 minutes longer, until the topping is golden and sizzling. Let the casserole stand for 20 minutes before serving.

MAKE AHEAD The casserole can be baked up to 4 hours ahead and served warm or at room temperature.

Breakfast & Brunch

Mom's Nutty Granola

Unlike most granolas, this one is more nutty than sweet; it has two kinds of nuts—almonds and peanuts—plus pumpkin and sunflower seeds. Jessamyn Waldman, founder of the nonprofit Hot Bread Kitchen at La Marqueta in East Harlem, New York, got the recipe from a home baker she admires: her mother, Nell Waldman.

INGREDIENTS

- 3 cups old-fashioned rolled oats
- ½ cup unsalted roasted peanuts
- ½ cup unsalted roasted almonds
- ½ cup unsalted roasted pumpkin seeds
- ½ cup unsalted roasted sunflower seeds
- ¼ cup wheat germ
- 1 teaspoon salt
- 1 tablespoon hot water
- ¾ cup honey
- ½ cup vegetable oil
- ½ cup raisins

MAKES 7 CUPS | TOTAL: 45 MIN PLUS COOLING

1 Preheat the oven to 325°. In a large bowl, toss the oats, nuts, seeds and wheat germ. In a small bowl, dissolve the salt in the hot water, then whisk in the honey and oil. Stir the liquid into the oat mixture to coat thoroughly, then spread on a large rimmed baking sheet.

2 Bake the granola in the center of the oven for 40 minutes, stirring every 10 minutes, until nearly dry. Turn off the oven and prop the door open halfway through baking; let the granola cool in the oven, stirring. Toss the granola with the raisins and serve.

SERVE WITH Sliced fresh fruit, fresh berries and milk or plain yogurt.

MAKE AHEAD The granola can be stored in an airtight container at room temperature for up to 3 weeks.

Ricotta Pancakes *with* Blueberries

Neal Fraser, chef-owner of the Los Angeles restaurants Grace and BLD (Breakfast Lunch Dinner), updates classic blueberry pancakes by adding fresh ricotta and beaten egg whites to the batter. They make the pancakes incredibly moist and light.

INGREDIENTS

1½ cups all-purpose flour

1 teaspoon baking powder

1½ teaspoons kosher salt

3 large eggs, separated

1¾ cups plus 2 tablespoons milk

6 ounces ricotta cheese (½ cup plus 2 tablespoons)

¼ cup sugar

1 tablespoon pure vanilla extract

Unsalted butter, for the griddle

1 pint fresh blueberries or 2 cups frozen blueberries, thawed

Pure maple syrup, for serving

6 SERVINGS | :) | TOTAL: 30 MIN

1 In a small bowl, whisk the flour with the baking powder and salt. In a large bowl, whisk the egg yolks with the milk, ricotta, sugar and vanilla. Add the dry ingredients and whisk until the batter is smooth.

2 In a large bowl, using an electric mixer, beat the egg whites at medium speed until frothy. Beat at high speed until soft peaks form. Fold the egg whites into the batter until no streaks remain.

3 Preheat the oven to 225°. Heat a griddle, then lightly butter it. For each pancake, ladle a scant ¼ cup of batter onto the griddle; be sure to leave enough space between the pancakes. Cook over moderately low heat until the bottoms are golden and the pancakes are just beginning to set, 1 to 2 minutes. Sprinkle each pancake with a few blueberries and press lightly. Flip the pancakes and cook until golden on the bottom and cooked through, about 1 minute longer. Transfer the pancakes to plates and keep them warm in the oven while you make the rest. Serve the pancakes with maple syrup.

MAKE AHEAD The batter can be covered and refrigerated overnight. Bring to room temperature and whisk briefly before cooking.

Yogurt-Zucchini Bread *with* Walnuts

In this variation on zucchini bread, FOOD & WINE's Grace Parisi uses thick Greek yogurt to add moisture without adding fat. As always, the bread is a terrific way to use up a bumper crop of late-summer zucchini.

INGREDIENTS

1 cup plus 2 tablespoons walnut halves
2 cups all-purpose flour
½ teaspoon baking powder
½ teaspoon baking soda
½ teaspoon salt

¾ cup plus 2 tablespoons sugar
2 large eggs
½ cup vegetable oil
½ cup fat-free plain Greek yogurt
1 cup coarsely grated zucchini (from about 1 medium zucchini)

MAKES ONE 9-INCH LOAF
ACTIVE: 15 MIN; TOTAL: 1 HR 30 MIN PLUS COOLING

1 Preheat the oven to 325°. Butter and flour a 9-by-4½-inch metal loaf pan. Spread the walnut halves in a pie plate and toast for about 8 minutes, until fragrant. Transfer the toasted walnuts to a cutting board and coarsely chop, then freeze for 5 minutes to cool.

2 In a large bowl, whisk the flour with the baking powder, baking soda and salt. In a medium bowl, mix the sugar with the eggs, oil and yogurt. Add the wet ingredients to the dry ingredients along with the grated zucchini and 1 cup of the toasted walnuts and stir until the batter is evenly moistened. Scrape the batter into the prepared pan and sprinkle the remaining 2 tablespoons of toasted walnuts on top. Bake for about 1 hour and 10 minutes, until the loaf is risen and a toothpick inserted in the center comes out clean. Let the loaf cool on a rack for 30 minutes before unmolding and serving.

MAKE AHEAD The zucchini loaf can be wrapped tightly in plastic and kept at room temperature for up to 4 days or wrapped tightly in plastic and foil and frozen for up to 1 month.

Fruit & Nut Energy Bars

At the Ranch at Rock Creek in Philipsburg, Montana, chef Josh Drage makes a luxe trail snack for the lodge's guests. In place of oats, peanuts and raisins, he opts for unexpected ingredients like kamut flakes (a whole-grain cereal), roasted cashews and dried figs and blueberries. And instead of honey, he uses agave nectar, which is lighter in flavor and less sweet.

INGREDIENTS

1 cup kamut flakes

1 cup pecans

½ cup salted roasted cashews

½ cup agave nectar

¼ cup smooth peanut butter

5 dried figs, stemmed and quartered

1 tablespoon flax seeds

1 tablespoon canola oil

Finely grated zest of 1 lemon

1 cup dried blueberries or currants

½ cup unsweetened coconut flakes

MAKES 1 DOZEN BARS | ☺ | ACTIVE: 15 MIN; TOTAL: 45 MIN

1 Preheat the oven to 325°. Line a large baking sheet with parchment paper. In a food processor, pulse the kamut, pecans, cashews, agave nectar, peanut butter, figs, flax seeds, canola oil and lemon zest until coarsely chopped. Add the dried blueberries and coconut flakes and pulse just until they are incorporated.

2 Scrape the mixture into a large bowl and stir well. Form the mixture into 12 bars or rounds ¾ inch thick and arrange them on the prepared baking sheet 1 inch apart. Bake for 25 minutes, until the bars are browned around the edges. Let the bars cool completely on the baking sheet before serving.

MAKE AHEAD The fruit-and-nut bars can be stored in an airtight container at room temperature for up to 5 days.

Butterscotch Sticky Buns

"I love adding glamour to old-school desserts," says Catherine Schimenti, the pastry chef at Michael Mina in San Francisco. She glazes these grown-up sticky buns with a sweet-salty butterscotch sauce spiked with Scotch instead of a white-sugar frosting. The result is "over-the-top, sticky, gooey goodness," she says.

INGREDIENTS

DOUGH

- ¾ cup whole milk
- 1 tablespoon plus ½ teaspoon active dry yeast
- ½ cup granulated sugar
- 1 stick unsalted butter— 6 tablespoons softened, 2 tablespoons melted
- 2 large eggs
- 4 cups all-purpose flour, plus more for dusting
- 1 teaspoon kosher salt
- 1 cup light brown sugar
- 2 teaspoons cinnamon
- 1 cup pecan halves

GLAZE

- ½ cup packed dark brown sugar
- 6 tablespoons unsalted butter
- 3 tablespoons Scotch whisky
- 2½ tablespoons sweetened condensed milk
- 2 tablespoons water
- 2 tablespoons crème fraîche
- 1½ teaspoons corn syrup
- ¼ teaspoon salt
- ⅛ teaspoon pure vanilla extract
- ⅛ teaspoon baking powder

MAKES 1 DOZEN BUNS | ACTIVE: 30 MIN; TOTAL: 2 HR 20 MIN

1 ***Make the dough*** In a glass measuring cup, microwave the milk until warm, 1 minute. In the bowl of a standing electric mixer fitted with the paddle, combine the warm milk and the yeast. Add the granulated sugar and softened butter and mix at medium speed until the butter is broken up, 1 minute. Beat in the eggs, one at a time. Add the 4 cups of flour and the salt; mix at low speed until incorporated, about 2 minutes. Scrape down the side of the bowl. Mix the dough at medium speed for 2 minutes longer. Scrape the dough into a lightly oiled bowl, cover with plastic wrap and let stand at room temperature for 30 minutes.

2 Preheat the oven to 325°. Spray a standard 12-cup muffin tin with nonstick cooking spray.

3 On a lightly floured surface, roll the dough out to a 9-by-24-inch rectangle. In a bowl, mix the light brown sugar with the cinnamon. Brush the melted butter over the dough; sprinkle with the cinnamon sugar. Beginning at a long edge, roll up the dough as tightly as possible; pinch the seam. Cut into twelve 2-inch pieces; set them in the muffin cups cut side up. Cover and let stand in a warm place for 30 minutes.

4 Set the muffin pan on a baking sheet and bake for 25 to 30 minutes, until the buns are golden brown. Spread the pecans in a pie plate and toast for 10 minutes, until fragrant. Let cool, then coarsely chop the nuts.

5 ***Make the glaze*** In a saucepan, bring the dark brown sugar, butter, Scotch, condensed milk, water, crème fraîche and corn syrup to a boil. Simmer over moderate heat until thickened slightly, 2 minutes. Remove from the heat; stir in the salt, vanilla and baking powder.

6 Unmold the buns. Pour the glaze over the hot buns and sprinkle with the pecans. Let stand for 20 minutes. Serve warm.

Cardamom-Spiced Crumb Cake

Most bakers spice their crumb cakes with cinnamon; for a more exotic flavor, FOOD & WINE's Kate Heddings tops her moist cake with a generous layer of cardamom-accented, pecan-dotted crumbs. The cake is easy to prepare (no electric mixer necessary) and makes a great hostess gift.

INGREDIENTS

CRUMB TOPPING
- 2 cups pecans
- 2 sticks (8 ounces) unsalted butter, melted
- ¾ cup light brown sugar
- ½ cup granulated sugar
- ½ teaspoon ground cardamom
- ½ teaspoon salt
- 2⅔ cups all-purpose flour

CAKE
- 3 cups all-purpose flour
- 1¼ cups granulated sugar
- 1½ teaspoons baking powder
- 1 teaspoon salt
- 2 large eggs
- 1 cup whole milk
- 1½ sticks (6 ounces) unsalted butter, melted
- 2 teaspoons pure vanilla extract

GLAZE
- ½ cup confectioners' sugar
- 2 tablespoons unsalted butter, melted
- 2 teaspoons whole milk
- ½ teaspoon pure vanilla extract

15 SERVINGS
ACTIVE: 30 MIN; TOTAL: 1 HR 30 MIN PLUS COOLING

1 Preheat the oven to 350°. Position a rack in the center of the oven. Butter a 13-by-9-inch metal baking pan.

2 **Make the crumb topping** Spread the pecans on a rimmed baking sheet and toast for 8 minutes, until browned. Let cool, then coarsely chop the nuts.

3 In a medium bowl, stir the melted butter with the light brown sugar, granulated sugar, cardamom and salt. Add the flour and stir until clumpy, then stir in the chopped nuts.

4 **Make the cake** In a large bowl, whisk the flour with the sugar, baking powder and salt. In a medium bowl, whisk the eggs with the milk, melted butter and vanilla. Add the egg mixture to the dry ingredients and stir until just combined. Scrape the batter into the prepared baking pan, smoothing the surface. Scatter the crumbs in large clumps over the cake; the crumb layer will be quite deep.

5 Bake for about 55 minutes, until the crumbs are golden and firm and a tester inserted in the center of the cake comes out clean. If the crumbs brown before the cake is done, cover the cake loosely with foil. Transfer to a rack to cool.

6 **Make the glaze** In a bowl, whisk all of the glaze ingredients together. Drizzle the glaze over the cake; let cool slightly. Serve warm or at room temperature.

MAKE AHEAD The cake can be kept covered at room temperature for up to 3 days.

Crème Fraîche Biscuits

In their French spin on Southern biscuits, husband-and-wife chefs Slade Rushing and Allison Vines-Rushing of MiLa in New Orleans replace buttermilk with crème fraîche and heavy cream. These decadent ingredients make the biscuits exceptionally fluffy.

INGREDIENTS

- 4 cups all-purpose flour, plus more for dusting
- 2 tablespoons baking powder
- 2 teaspoons kosher salt
- 1 teaspoon sugar

- 2 sticks (8 ounces) cold unsalted butter, cut into tablespoons
- 1¼ cups heavy cream
- ½ cup crème fraîche
- 1 large egg

MAKES ABOUT 22 BISCUITS
ACTIVE: 20 MIN; TOTAL: 1 HR 10 MIN

1 Preheat the oven to 400°. In a large bowl, whisk the 4 cups of flour with the baking powder, salt and sugar. Cut in the butter until it's the size of peas. Make a well in the center.

2 In a small bowl, whisk the heavy cream with the crème fraîche and egg and pour into the well. Stir with a fork until evenly moistened. Turn the dough out onto a lightly floured work surface and gently knead 2 or 3 times until it holds together.

3 Roll out the dough 1 inch thick. Using a 2¼-inch round cookie cutter, stamp out the biscuits as close together as possible. Gently press the scraps together and stamp out more biscuits. Transfer to baking sheets and refrigerate until firm, about 30 minutes.

4 Bake the biscuits for 18 minutes, or until golden on top. Serve warm from the oven or at room temperature.

MAKE AHEAD The biscuits can be kept in an airtight container overnight; rewarm before serving.

Scrambled Eggs *with* Herbed Croutons

FOOD & WINE's Grace Parisi creates a witty take on scrambled eggs and toast by stirring delicious herbed croutons right into her soft, creamy eggs.

INGREDIENTS

4 slices of multigrain bread (about 5 ounces), crusts removed and bread cut into ½-inch cubes

¼ cup extra-virgin olive oil

2 garlic cloves, lightly smashed

2 thyme sprigs

One 2-inch rosemary sprig

Salt and freshly ground pepper

1 tablespoon unsalted butter

10 large eggs, beaten

2 tablespoons snipped chives

4 SERVINGS | TOTAL: 25 MIN

1 In a medium bowl, toss the bread cubes with the olive oil, garlic and herb sprigs. Transfer to a large nonstick skillet and cook over moderate heat, stirring, until the bread is crisp and browned and the herbs are frizzled, about 10 minutes. Transfer the croutons to a plate and discard the garlic. Finely chop the herbs and add them to the croutons; season with salt and pepper.

2 Wipe out the skillet and melt the butter in it. Season the eggs with salt and pepper and add them to the skillet. Cook over moderate heat, stirring gently with a rubber spatula, until the eggs are partially set, about 2 minutes. Add the croutons and chives and gently fold them in, cooking the eggs to soft curds, about 1 minute longer. Transfer the eggs to plates and serve right away.

Roquefort Soufflés

Most cheese soufflés call for Gruyère; *Top Chef* judge and FOOD & WINE special-projects director Gail Simmons updates the recipe by using a mix of creamy Roquefort and tangy Parmigiano-Reggiano (Fontina or goat cheese would also be good). To make certain her soufflés rise, she folds lots of fluffy whipped egg whites into the cheesy, chive-speckled base.

Fluffy soufflés and other egg-based dishes call for equally light or even sparkling wines. Two choices from Spain: an Albariño like the minerally 2009 Burgans or a cava like the lemony 2007 Raventós i Blanc L'Hereu Reserva Brut.

INGREDIENTS

- 2 tablespoons unsalted butter, plus softened butter for the ramekins
- ½ cup freshly grated Parmigiano-Reggiano cheese
- 3 tablespoons all-purpose flour
- 1 cup milk

- Pinch of salt
- Pinch of cayenne pepper
- 2 ounces Roquefort cheese
- 5 large eggs, separated
- 2 tablespoons snipped chives

4 SERVINGS | ☺ | TOTAL: 40 MIN

1 Preheat the oven to 375°. Butter four 1-cup ramekins and coat each one with 1 tablespoon of the grated Parmigiano.

2 In a medium saucepan, melt the 2 tablespoons of butter. Add the flour and cook over moderate heat for 1 minute, whisking constantly. Add the milk, salt and cayenne and cook, whisking, until very thick and bubbling, about 2 minutes. Scrape the mixture into a large bowl and whisk in the Roquefort and the remaining ¼ cup of grated Parmigiano. Whisk in the egg yolks and chives.

3 In another bowl, using an electric mixer, beat the egg whites until firm peaks form. Fold the beaten whites into the cheese mixture until no streaks remain. Pour the mixture into the ramekins, filling them three-fourths of the way; set the ramekins on a baking sheet. Bake the soufflés for about 20 minutes, until they are puffed and golden. Place the cheese soufflés on plates and serve immediately.

SERVE WITH Mixed green salad.

Desserts

Berry-Yogurt Pavlovas *with* Chamomile-Lavender Syrup

Beloved in Australia and New Zealand, the pavlova is a baked meringue served with whipped cream and fruit. FOOD & WINE's Melissa Rubel Jacobson updates the classic and makes it healthier by topping the meringues with Greek yogurt instead of whipped cream, then spooning on berries flavored with lavender and chamomile.

※ *Delicate, slightly effervescent Moscato goes extremely well with most light fruit desserts, such as these cloudlike pavlovas. Try the peachy 2009 St. Supéry Moscato or the floral 2008 Tintero Moscato d'Asti.*

INGREDIENTS

- 3 large egg whites
- ⅛ teaspoon cream of tartar
- 1¼ cups sugar
- ½ cup water
- 1 chamomile tea bag
- ¼ teaspoon dried lavender buds (see Note)

- 1¼ cups raspberries
- ¾ cup blueberries
- ½ cup blackberries
- 1 cup 2-percent plain Greek yogurt

4 SERVINGS | ACTIVE: 30 MIN; TOTAL: 2 HR 30 MIN

1 Preheat the oven to 250° and position a rack in the lower third. Line a baking sheet with parchment paper.

2 In a bowl, beat the egg whites with the cream of tartar at medium speed until frothy. Beat in ¾ cup of the sugar, 1 tablespoon at a time, until the meringue is thick and glossy; scoop into four 4½-inch mounds onto the prepared baking sheet. Using the back of a spoon, make a well in the center of each mound; bake for 1 hour, until crisp but still chewy inside. Turn off the oven and prop the door open; let the meringues cool for 1 hour.

3 Meanwhile, in a saucepan, combine the remaining ½ cup of sugar and the water and bring to a boil; remove from the heat. Add the chamomile tea bag and lavender and let stand for 10 minutes. Strain the syrup into a bowl. Let stand until the syrup is cool.

4 In a bowl, gently toss all of the berries with ¼ cup of the chamomile-lavender syrup. Top the meringues with the yogurt and berries, drizzle with the remaining syrup and serve.

NOTE Dried lavender buds are available at specialty food shops.

Mixed-Berry Spoon Cake

To spice up a basic spoon cake, FOOD & WINE's Grace Parisi adds candied ginger to the mixed berries. To make the cake with other seasonal fillings, she suggests replacing the berries with 4 pounds of stone fruit (peaches, nectarines and apricots), cut into large wedges; 4 pounds of plums, cut into 1-inch cubes; or 6 pints of blueberries plus 2 tablespoons of fresh lemon juice.

INGREDIENTS

FILLING

- 4 pints strawberries (2 pounds), hulled and quartered
- 2 pints blackberries (12 ounces)
- 2 pints raspberries (12 ounces)
- 1 tablespoon minced candied ginger
- ¾ cup sugar
- 2 tablespoons cornstarch

BATTER

- 1½ cups all-purpose flour
- 1 cup sugar
- 2 teaspoons finely grated lemon zest
- 1½ teaspoons baking powder
- 1 teaspoon kosher salt
- 2 eggs
- ½ cup milk
- 1 teaspoon pure vanilla extract
- 1½ sticks (6 ounces) unsalted butter, melted

8 TO 10 SERVINGS | ACTIVE: 20 MIN; TOTAL: 2 HR 20 MIN

1 ***Make the filling*** In a large bowl, gently toss the strawberries, blackberries, raspberries and candied ginger with the sugar and cornstarch; let stand for 10 minutes.

2 ***Meanwhile, make the batter*** Preheat the oven to 375°. In a medium bowl, whisk the flour with the sugar, lemon zest, baking powder and salt. In a small bowl, whisk the eggs with the milk and vanilla. Whisk the liquid into the dry ingredients until evenly moistened, then whisk in the melted butter until smooth.

3 Spread the filling in a 13-by-9-inch baking dish. Spoon the batter on top, leaving small gaps. Bake in the center of the oven for 1 hour, until the fruit is bubbling and a toothpick inserted into the topping comes out clean. Let the cake cool for 1 hour before serving.

MAKE AHEAD The spoon cake can be made ahead and kept at room temperature for up to 6 hours.

Deep-Dish Strawberry-Rhubarb Pie

Many cooks claim lard makes the best pie crusts, but for years, FOOD & WINE's Grace Parisi insisted on butter alone because the only lard available was the heavily processed and unpleasant-tasting kind sold in supermarkets. Now that excellent small-batch lard is sold at farmers' markets and good butcher shops, however, she swaps in fresh leaf lard—the creamy white fat that surrounds a hog's kidneys—for some of the butter. It yields an incredibly flaky crust with a rich flavor.

INGREDIENTS

DOUGH
2½ cups all-purpose flour
½ teaspoon salt
1½ sticks (6 ounces) cold unsalted butter, cut into ½-inch dice
¼ cup lard (2 ounces), frozen and cut into ½-inch cubes
½ cup ice water

FILLING
1½ pounds strawberries, hulled and quartered (5 cups)
1½ pounds rhubarb, sliced ½ inch thick (5 cups)
1 cup sugar, plus more for sprinkling
¼ cup cornstarch
Pinch of salt

MAKES ONE 9½-INCH DEEP-DISH PIE
ACTIVE: 50 MIN; TOTAL: 3 HR PLUS COOLING

1 **Make the dough** In a food processor, pulse the flour with the salt. Add the cold butter and frozen lard and pulse 5 or 6 times, until the pieces are the size of peas. Drizzle on the ice water and pulse just until the crumbs are moistened.

2 Press the dough into a ball. Divide the dough into 2 pieces, one slightly smaller than the other. Flatten into disks, wrap in plastic and refrigerate until firm, at least 30 minutes.

3 **Make the filling** Preheat the oven to 375° and position a rack in the lower third. In a bowl, toss the strawberries and rhubarb with the 1 cup of sugar, the cornstarch and the salt.

4 Roll out the larger piece of dough to a 13-inch round about ⅛ inch thick. Line a 9½-by-1¾-inch glass pie plate with the dough. Brush the overhang with water and spoon in the filling.

5 Roll out the smaller piece of dough to a 12-inch round and lay it over the filling; press the edges together. Trim the overhang to ½ inch, fold it under itself and crimp. Lightly brush the top with water and sprinkle with sugar. Cut a few slits for steam to escape.

6 Bake the pie until the filling is bubbling and the crust is golden brown, about 2 hours. Cover the edge of the pie with aluminum foil if it begins to darken during baking. Let the pie cool for about 5 hours at room temperature before serving.

MAKE AHEAD The pie can be kept at room temperature overnight. Rewarm in a 325° oven for 15 minutes if desired.

Apple Pie Bars

Capturing the flavors of apple pie in a snack bar is a fantastic idea; the bars here have a nutty, streusel-like topping and a crisp shortbread bottom. This dessert is on the menu at L.A.'s Big Sugar Bakeshop courtesy of Cathy Johnson, co-owner Mary Odson's sister.

INGREDIENTS

CRUST
- 3 sticks (12 ounces) unsalted butter, softened
- ¾ cup granulated sugar
- 3 cups all-purpose flour
- ½ teaspoon kosher salt

FILLING
- 6 tablespoons unsalted butter
- ½ cup light brown sugar
- 12 Granny Smith apples (about 6 pounds)—peeled, cored and thinly sliced
- 1 tablespoon cinnamon

- ¼ teaspoon freshly grated nutmeg
- 1 cup water, as necessary

TOPPING
- ¾ cup walnuts
- 3 cups quick-cooking oats
- 2 cups all-purpose flour
- 1½ cups light brown sugar
- 1¼ teaspoons cinnamon
- ½ teaspoon baking soda
- ½ teaspoon kosher salt
- 3 sticks (12 ounces) unsalted butter, cut into ½-inch cubes and chilled

---

MAKES 4 DOZEN 2-INCH BARS | ACTIVE: 1 HR; TOTAL: 2 HR

1 **Make the crust** Preheat the oven to 375°. Line a 17-by-15-inch rimmed baking sheet or jelly roll pan with parchment paper. In a standing electric mixer fitted with the paddle, beat the butter with the granulated sugar at medium speed until light and fluffy, about 2 minutes. At low speed, beat in the flour and salt until a soft dough forms. Press the dough over the bottom of the prepared pan and ½ inch up the sides in an even layer. Bake in the center of the oven for about 20 minutes, until the crust is golden and set. Let cool on a rack.

2 **Meanwhile, make the filling** In each of 2 large skillets, melt 3 tablespoons of the butter with ¼ cup of the light brown sugar. Add the apples to the skillets and cook over high heat, stirring occasionally, until softened, about 10 minutes. Stir half of the cinnamon and nutmeg into each skillet. Cook until the apples are caramelized and very tender and the liquid is evaporated, about 10 minutes longer; scrape up any bits stuck to the bottom of the skillets; add up to ½ cup of water to each pan to prevent scorching. Let cool.

3 **Make the topping** Spread the walnuts in a pie plate; toast until golden, about 8 minutes. Let cool, then coarsely chop. In a bowl, mix the oats, flour, light brown sugar, cinnamon, baking soda and salt. Using a pastry blender or 2 knives, cut in the butter until the mixture resembles coarse meal. Stir in the walnuts; press the mixture into clumps.

4 Spread the apple filling over the crust. Scatter the crumbs on top, pressing lightly into an even layer. Bake in the center of the oven for 1 hour, until the topping is golden; rotate the pan halfway through baking. Let cool completely on a rack before cutting into 2-inch bars. **MAKE AHEAD** The bars can be stored in an airtight container at room temperature for 4 days or frozen for up to 1 month.

Pear Tarte Tatin *with* Red Wine Caramel

Classic tarte Tatin is made with apples. Shawn McClain, chef-partner at Sage in Las Vegas, makes a pear version and adds spiced red wine to the caramel sauce. Because his recipe calls for store-bought puff pastry (McClain is a huge fan of Dufour's), it's quite easy to prepare.

INGREDIENTS

2 cups dry red wine

2 cinnamon sticks

½ cup sugar

¼ cup water

2 tablespoons unsalted butter

1 tablespoon pear liqueur (optional)

5 firm, ripe Bartlett pears— peeled, cored and halved

One 14-ounce sheet all-butter puff pastry, chilled

Crème fraîche, for serving

8 TO 10 SERVINGS | ACTIVE: 30 MIN; TOTAL: 3 HR

1 In a small saucepan, boil the wine with the cinnamon sticks over moderately high heat until the wine is reduced to ¼ cup, about 15 minutes. Discard the cinnamon sticks.

2 In a 12-inch ovenproof skillet, combine the sugar and water. Cook over moderately high heat, swirling the pan occasionally, until a light amber caramel forms, about 5 minutes. Remove from the heat. Add the red wine syrup along with the butter and liqueur, then cook over moderately high heat to dissolve the hardened caramel, about 1 minute. Add the pears to the skillet and cook over low heat, turning occasionally, until the pears are tender and the pan juices are syrupy, about 20 minutes. Arrange the pears cut side up in the skillet with the narrow ends pointing toward the center. Let cool for 30 minutes.

3 Preheat the oven to 375°. On a lightly floured work surface, roll out the pastry to a 13-inch square. Using the skillet lid as a template, cut out a 12-inch round piece of pastry. Cut four 2-inch-long steam vents in the pastry and lay it over the pears, tucking the edge into the skillet. Bake for about 1 hour and 10 minutes, until the pastry is deeply golden and risen. Let the tart cool in the skillet for 15 minutes, then very carefully invert it onto a large plate. Cut the tart into wedges and serve with crème fraîche.

Bourbon-Spiked Pumpkin Pie

FOOD & WINE's Grace Parisi likes to fortify her pumpkin pie with a splash of bourbon. Then she tops it with pumpkins she makes with leftover dough. To create your own decoration, roll out the dough, cut out shapes using a knife or cookie cutter and bake on a separate sheet. Be sure to watch closely—small pieces bake quickly.

INGREDIENTS

DOUGH

1¼ cups all-purpose flour, plus more for rolling

Pinch of salt

1 stick (4 ounces) cold unsalted butter, cubed

¼ cup ice water

FILLING

4 large eggs

¾ cup sugar

1 tablespoon cornstarch

2 teaspoons cinnamon

¼ teaspoon cloves

Pinch of salt

One 15-ounce can pumpkin puree

½ cup heavy cream

2 tablespoons bourbon

MAKES ONE 9-INCH PIE
ACTIVE: 30 MIN; TOTAL: 3 HR PLUS COOLING

1 **Make the dough** In a food processor, pulse the 1¼ cups of flour with the salt. Add the butter and pulse until the pieces are the size of peas. Drizzle in the ice water and pulse until the crumbs are moistened; turn out onto a work surface. Gather into a ball, flatten, wrap in plastic and refrigerate for 30 minutes.

2 Preheat the oven to 350°. On a lightly floured work surface, roll out the pie dough to a 13-inch round a scant ¼ inch thick. Fit the dough into a 9-inch glass pie plate and trim the overhang to ¾ inch. Fold the dough under itself and crimp decoratively, then refrigerate the pie shell for 10 minutes.

3 Line the pie shell with foil and fill with pie weights or dried beans. Bake in the center of the oven until nearly set, about 25 minutes. Remove the foil and weights and bake until the crust is pale golden, about 10 minutes. Let cool slightly.

4 **Make the filling** In a medium bowl, whisk the eggs with the sugar, cornstarch, cinnamon, cloves and salt until smooth. Whisk in the pumpkin puree, then the cream and bourbon. Working near the oven, pour the filling into the crust. Bake for about 45 minutes, until the custard is set. Let the pie cool on a rack, then serve.

MAKE AHEAD The pie can be refrigerated for up to 1 day. Let return to room temperature before serving.

Carrot Cake *with* Fluffy Cream Cheese Frosting

Carrot cake, that 1970s favorite, is now a fixture on fancy restaurant menus. While at Urban Farmer in Portland, Oregon, pastry chef Jodi Elliott prepared a version using buttermilk and a full pound of carrots. It's especially moist, dense and not too sweet.

INGREDIENTS

CAKE

- 1 cup pecans
- 2 cups all-purpose flour, plus more for the pans
- 2 teaspoons baking powder
- 2 teaspoons baking soda
- 1 teaspoon cinnamon
- 1 teaspoon salt
- 1 cup vegetable oil
- ½ cup buttermilk
- 1½ teaspoons pure vanilla extract
- 4 large eggs
- 2 cups granulated sugar
- 1 pound carrots, peeled and coarsely shredded

FROSTING

- 2 sticks (8 ounces) unsalted butter, softened
- Two 8-ounce packages cream cheese, softened
- 1 tablespoon pure vanilla extract
- 2 cups confectioners' sugar

8 TO 10 SERVINGS | ACTIVE: 40 MIN; TOTAL: 3 HR 30 MIN

1 Preheat the oven to 325°. Butter two 9-inch cake pans; line the bottoms with parchment paper. Butter the paper and flour the pans.

2 **Make the cake** Spread the pecans on a baking sheet and toast for 8 minutes, until fragrant. Cool and finely chop the pecans.

3 In a medium bowl, whisk the 2 cups of flour with the baking powder, baking soda, cinnamon and salt. In a small bowl, whisk the oil with the buttermilk and vanilla. In a large bowl, using an electric mixer, beat the eggs and granulated sugar at high speed until pale, 5 minutes. Beat in the liquid ingredients. Beat in the dry ingredients just until moistened. Stir in the carrots and pecans. Divide the batter between the pans and bake the cakes for 55 minutes to 1 hour, until springy and golden. Let the cakes cool on a rack for 30 minutes, then unmold the cakes and let cool completely.

4 **Make the frosting** In a large bowl, using an electric mixer, beat the softened butter and cream cheese at high speed until light, about 5 minutes. Beat in the vanilla extract, then the confectioners' sugar; beat at low speed until incorporated. Increase the speed to high and beat until light and fluffy, about 3 minutes.

5 Peel off the parchment paper and invert one cake layer onto a plate. Spread with a slightly rounded cup of the frosting. Top with the second cake layer, right side up. Spread the top and side of the cake with the remaining frosting and refrigerate until chilled, about 1 hour. Slice the cake and serve.

MAKE AHEAD The frosted cake can be refrigerated for up to 1 day.

Lemon-Blueberry Cheesecake Parfaits

This reimagined cheesecake from Maggie Leung, the pastry chef at Masa's in San Francisco, is very versatile. The cheesecake custard and blueberry compote are delicious with the buttery shortbread cookies here, but you can also eat the custard with fresh fruit or drizzle the compote over ice cream.

INGREDIENTS

BLUEBERRY COMPOTE
- 2 cups blueberries (12 ounces)
- ¼ cup sugar
- ¼ cup water
- 1 teaspoon fresh lemon juice

CHEESECAKE CUSTARD
- 1 cup whole milk
- 5 tablespoons sugar
- 4 large egg yolks
- 2½ tablespoons cornstarch

- 6 ounces cream cheese, at room temperature
- ¼ cup plus 2 tablespoons fresh lemon juice
- 1 teaspoon finely grated lemon zest, plus extra strips for garnish
- 1 teaspoon pure vanilla extract
- 1 cup heavy cream
- 1 pound shortbread cookies, broken into ½-inch pieces

8 SERVINGS | ACTIVE: 30 MIN; TOTAL: 2 HR 20 MIN

1 *Make the blueberry compote* In a saucepan, combine 1 cup of the blueberries with the sugar and water. Bring to a simmer and cook over moderate heat until the blueberries break down, about 5 minutes. Scrape the blueberry sauce into a blender, add the lemon juice and puree until smooth. Scrape the sauce into a bowl, fold in the remaining 1 cup of whole blueberries and refrigerate until chilled, about 2 hours.

2 *Meanwhile, make the cheesecake custard* In a saucepan, bring ¾ cup of the milk to a boil with 3 tablespoons of the sugar; remove from the heat. In a bowl, whisk the egg yolks with the cornstarch and the remaining ¼ cup of milk and 2 tablespoons of sugar. Gradually whisk the hot milk into the egg yolks, then pour the mixture back into the saucepan and whisk constantly over moderate heat until thickened, about 2 minutes. Over low heat, whisk in the cream cheese, lemon juice, grated lemon zest and vanilla until smooth, about 1 minute. Scrape into a bowl. Press a piece of plastic wrap directly onto the surface of the custard and refrigerate until chilled, about 2 hours.

3 In a bowl, using an electric mixer, beat the heavy cream to medium peaks. Fold the whipped cream into the chilled cheesecake custard until no streaks remain. Spoon the shortbread pieces and cheesecake custard into bowls. Drizzle with the blueberry compote, garnish with the lemon zest strips and serve.

MAKE AHEAD The assembled parfaits can be refrigerated for up to 1 day.

Pecan-Praline Cheesecake *with* Caramel Sauce

The crust for this airy cheesecake from Lisa Ritter, co-owner of L.A.'s Big Sugar Bakeshop, is inspired by pralines (candy made from nuts and caramelized sugar). Although slightly more time-intensive than a plain graham-cracker crust, it's worth the extra effort, as is the buttery caramel sauce poured on top.

This caramelly, nutty cheesecake would be great with a rich dessert wine like port, which has enough acidity to prevent the pairing from being cloying. Try the cocoa-scented NV Quinta do Infantado Tawny or Warre's Otima 10-Year-Old Tawny.

INGREDIENTS

CRUST
- ½ cup pecan halves
- 1 stick plus ½ teaspoon unsalted butter, melted
- ⅓ cup plus ½ tablespoon granulated sugar
- 2 tablespoons light brown sugar
- 1½ tablespoons heavy cream
- Pinch of salt
- 2 packets graham crackers (about 10 ounces), crushed

FILLING
- 1 pound full-fat cream cheese, softened
- 1 cup granulated sugar
- 3 large eggs
- 1 teaspoon pure vanilla extract
- 24 ounces full-fat sour cream

CARAMEL SAUCE
- 4 tablespoons unsalted butter, softened
- 2 tablespoons granulated sugar
- 2 tablespoons light brown sugar
- ⅓ cup dark brown sugar
- ½ cup heavy cream
- ¼ teaspoon pure vanilla extract
- ¼ teaspoon salt

16 SERVINGS | TOTAL: 2 HR PLUS OVERNIGHT CHILLING

1 **Make the crust** Preheat the oven to 375°. Line a baking sheet with parchment paper. Wrap the outside of a 10-inch round springform pan with foil. In a bowl, toss the pecans with ½ teaspoon of the butter, ½ tablespoon of the granulated sugar, the brown sugar, cream and salt. Spread the nuts on the baking sheet and bake for about 18 minutes, until the sugar is caramelized and the pecans are toasted. Let cool.

2 Transfer all but 12 of the pecans to a food processor along with the graham crackers and pulse until fine. Add the remaining melted butter and ⅓ cup of granulated sugar and pulse until the crumbs are moistened. Press the crumbs over the bottom and two-thirds up the side of the prepared pan.

3 **Make the filling** In a clean food processor, pulse the cream cheese and sugar until smooth. Add the eggs, one at a time, and pulse until incorporated. Pulse in the vanilla and sour cream. Scrape the filling into the pan and bake for about 1 hour, until the top of the cheesecake is lightly golden in spots and the center is slightly jiggly. Transfer the cheesecake to a rack and let cool completely. Wrap in plastic and refrigerate overnight.

4 **Make the caramel sauce** In a medium saucepan, combine the butter with the sugars and bring to a boil, stirring constantly. Cook over moderately high heat for 2 minutes, stirring constantly. Add the cream and boil for 2 minutes. Transfer to a pitcher. Stir in the vanilla and salt and refrigerate until cold, at least 2 hours or overnight.

5 Unwrap the cheesecake and discard the foil. Remove the ring and transfer the cake to a plate. Arrange the 12 reserved pecans on top. Using a warm, slightly moistened knife, cut the cake into wedges, wiping and rewetting the blade between slices. Transfer to plates and pour some of the caramel on top. Serve with the remaining sauce.

Coconut Arborio Rice Pudding

In place of the medium-grain or basmati rice typically used in rice puddings, pastry chef Stephanie Prida of Chicago's Elysian hotel opts for arborio, commonly used for risotto. The plump grains give her coconut-infused pudding a supercreamy texture while staying perfectly firm and chewy.

INGREDIENTS

1 quart whole milk
1 cup arborio rice (about 8 ounces)
½ cup sugar
2 cups water

One 14-ounce can unsweetened coconut milk
½ cup coarsely shredded unsweetened coconut

6 SERVINGS | TOTAL: 45 MIN

1 In a large saucepan, combine the milk, rice, sugar and water and bring to a boil. Simmer over moderate heat, stirring frequently, until the rice is tender and suspended in a thick, creamy sauce, about 30 minutes. Stir in the coconut milk and simmer, stirring occasionally, until the rice is very tender and the liquid is thickened, about 10 minutes. Let cool slightly.

2 Meanwhile, in a medium saucepan, toast the coconut over moderate heat, stirring constantly, until fragrant and golden, about 4 minutes. Transfer to a plate to cool.

3 Spoon the rice pudding into bowls, garnish with the toasted coconut and serve.

Lemon Meringue Cupcakes

By adding lemon juice and zest to marshmallow frosting, then spreading it on moist golden cupcakes and briefly broiling them, FOOD & WINE's Grace Parisi adds lemon-meringue-pie flavor to a basic sweet.

✳ *Vin santo is a classic Tuscan sweet wine that usually has some orange and other citrusy flavors alongside its nutty, honeyed notes, making it a great match for these lemony cupcakes. Look for the 2004 Badia a Coltibuono or the 2002 Villa la Selva Vigna del Papa.*

INGREDIENTS

CUPCAKES

- 1 cup plus 2 tablespoons all-purpose flour
- 2 tablespoons cornstarch
- 1¼ teaspoons baking powder
- ⅛ teaspoon salt
- ¾ cup sugar
- 2 large eggs, at room temperature
- 1¼ teaspoons pure vanilla extract
- 4 tablespoons unsalted butter, melted
- ¼ cup vegetable oil
- ½ cup milk, at room temperature

FROSTING

- 1 cup sugar
- 3 tablespoons water
- 2 large egg whites, at room temperature
- Pinch of cream of tartar
- Pinch of salt
- ½ teaspoon finely grated lemon zest
- 1 tablespoon fresh lemon juice

MAKES 1 DOZEN CUPCAKES | TOTAL: 1 HR

---

1 ***Make the cupcakes*** Preheat the oven to 350°. Line a 12-cup muffin tin with paper or foil liners.

2 In a medium bowl, whisk the flour with the cornstarch, baking powder and salt. In a large bowl, using a handheld electric mixer, beat the sugar with the eggs and vanilla extract at medium-high speed until smooth and slightly thickened, about 3 minutes. Add the butter and oil and beat until incorporated, scraping the bottom and side of the bowl. Add the dry ingredients and milk in 3 alternating batches, beating well between additions. Carefully pour the batter into the lined muffin tins, filling them about two-thirds full.

3 Bake in the center of the oven for 20 to 23 minutes, until the cupcakes are springy and a toothpick or cake tester inserted in the center comes out clean. Let the cupcakes cool slightly in the muffin tin, then transfer them to a wire rack to cool completely.

4 ***Meanwhile, make the frosting*** In a small saucepan, combine the sugar with the water and bring to a boil over moderately high heat, stirring constantly, until the sugar has dissolved, 2 to 3 minutes.

5 In a large bowl of a standing electric mixer, beat the egg whites with the cream of tartar and salt until soft peaks form. With the mixer at medium speed, carefully pour the hot sugar syrup into the egg whites. Continue beating the frosting until cool and billowy, about 5 minutes. Add the lemon zest and juice and beat until combined.

6 Preheat the broiler. Spread the frosting on the cooled cupcakes. Transfer the cupcakes to a baking sheet and broil for 30 seconds, or until the frosting is browned in spots, then serve.

MAKE AHEAD The unfrosted cupcakes can be wrapped in plastic and stored at room temperature for up to 2 days or frozen for up to 1 month.

Roll & Cut Sugar Cookies

These cookies from baking teacher and cookbook author Cindy Mushet are a classic, especially when they're sprinkled with confectioners' sugar or sandwiched with apricot jam, as in the photo here. But the recipe is also amazing with elderflower or gooseberry jam. Or spread the cookies with Nutella.

INGREDIENTS

2¼ cups all-purpose flour

¾ cup sugar

¼ teaspoon salt

2 sticks (8 ounces) cold unsalted butter, cut into ½-inch pieces

2 large egg yolks

2 teaspoons pure vanilla extract

¾ cup seedless raspberry, apricot, elderflower or gooseberry jam (for jam-filled cookies)

Royal Icing (recipe follows), dragées, sprinkles and confectioners' sugar, for decorating

MAKES ABOUT 4 DOZEN 3 TO 4-INCH COOKIES, OR 2 DOZEN SANDWICH COOKIES | ACTIVE: 1 HR; TOTAL: 3 HR

1 In the bowl of a standing electric mixer fitted with the paddle, mix the flour, sugar and salt. Add the butter; mix at low speed until the butter is broken up into small pieces, about 2 minutes. Increase the speed to medium and mix until the flour and butter form small clumps, about 1 minute. Add the egg yolks and vanilla; mix at low speed until the dough comes together in a few large clumps. Pat the dough into two ½-inch-thick disks, wrap in plastic and refrigerate until chilled but not firm, about 30 minutes.

2 Preheat the oven to 375°. Line 2 large rimmed baking sheets with parchment paper. On a lightly floured surface, working with one disk at a time, roll out the dough ⅛ inch thick. Using 3- to 4-inch cookie cutters, cut the dough into shapes and transfer to the prepared baking sheets. (Alternatively, cut the dough into 3- to 4-inch shapes and, using a smaller cutter, stamp out the centers of half of the cookies.) Reroll the scraps and cut out more cookies. Refrigerate the cookies until chilled, about 30 minutes.

3 Bake the cookies for about 13 minutes, until lightly golden around the edges; shift the baking sheets halfway through. Let the cookies cool on the baking sheets for about 5 minutes, then carefully transfer to a rack to cool completely, about 20 minutes.

4 For sandwich cookies, spread a thin layer of jam on the solid cookies and top with the corresponding cutout cookies. Or decorate with the icing, sprinkles, confectioners' sugar and dragées.

Royal Icing

MAKES ABOUT 1¼ CUPS | ⟳ | TOTAL: 10 MIN

In a bowl, beat 1 egg white at medium speed until foamy. Add ½ pound (2¼ cups) confectioners' sugar 1 cup at a time, beating between additions, until completely incorporated. Add 1 tablespoon water; beat at high speed until the icing holds its shape, about 5 minutes. Spoon into a piping bag fitted with a plain tip and use at once; thin with water if necessary.

Ganache-Stuffed Chocolate Chip Cookies

Jessica Sullivan, the pastry chef at Boulevard restaurant in San Francisco, combines two dessert basics—nutty chocolate chip cookies and silky chocolate ganache—into one heavenly sandwich cookie. Sullivan likes hers stuffed (not merely spread) with ganache. If you're the kind of person who twists apart sandwich cookies to get to the filling, you'll want your cookies stuffed, too.

INGREDIENTS

COOKIES
- 1 cup walnuts
- 1 cup plus 2 tablespoons all-purpose flour
- 1 teaspoon baking soda
- ½ teaspoon salt
- 1 stick (4 ounces) unsalted butter, at room temperature
- ½ cup packed light brown sugar
- ¼ cup granulated sugar
- ½ teaspoon pure vanilla extract
- 1 large egg
- 1 cup bittersweet chocolate chips

GANACHE
- 4 ounces bittersweet chocolate, chopped
- 5 tablespoons heavy cream
- 2½ tablespoons light corn syrup
- 2 tablespoons crème fraîche

MAKES 18 STUFFED COOKIES | ACTIVE: 45 MIN; TOTAL: 2 HR

1 **Make the cookies** Preheat the oven to 375°. Spread the nuts in a pie plate and toast for 8 minutes; let cool, then chop.

2 In a bowl, mix the flour, baking soda and salt. In the bowl of a standing mixer fitted with the paddle (or using a handheld mixer), cream the butter with the sugars and vanilla at medium speed, about 1 minute. Beat in the egg. With the mixer at low speed, beat in the dry ingredients. Beat in the walnuts and chocolate chips. Spoon level tablespoons of the dough onto 2 ungreased baking sheets, about 2 inches apart. Refrigerate for 30 minutes, until firm.

3 **Make the ganache** Put the chopped chocolate in a bowl. In a saucepan, bring the cream and corn syrup to a boil; pour over the chocolate and let stand for 1 minute. Whisk until smooth. Whisk in the crème fraîche. Refrigerate the ganache, stirring occasionally, until thick and spreadable, 1 hour.

4 Bake the cookies for 12 minutes, until golden; let cool on the baking sheets for 2 minutes, then transfer to a rack to cool completely.

5 Sandwich the cookies with the chocolate ganache and serve.
MAKE AHEAD The stuffed chocolate chip cookies can be stored in an airtight container at room temperature for up to 3 days.

Salted Fudge Brownies

For the past several years, pastry chefs and home bakers have been experimenting with salty flavors in desserts. Here, FOOD & WINE's Kate Krader adds an extra touch of salt to her classic fudge brownies. She recommends a flaky sea salt like Maldon, because the flavor is mild and the salt melts so nicely into the batter.

INGREDIENTS

1½ sticks (6 ounces) unsalted butter

2 ounces unsweetened chocolate, finely chopped

¼ cup plus 2 tablespoons unsweetened cocoa powder

2 cups sugar

3 large eggs

1½ teaspoons pure vanilla extract

1 cup all-purpose flour

½ teaspoon Maldon sea salt, plus more for sprinkling (optional)

MAKES 16 BROWNIES | TOTAL: 45 MIN PLUS 2 HR COOLING

1 Preheat the oven to 350°. Line a 9-inch square metal cake pan with foil, draping the foil over the edges. Lightly butter the foil.

2 In a large saucepan, melt the butter with the unsweetened chocolate over very low heat, stirring occasionally. Remove from the heat. Whisking them in one at a time until thoroughly incorporated, add the unsweetened cocoa, sugar, eggs, vanilla extract and flour. Pour the batter into the prepared cake pan and smooth the surface. Sprinkle the ½ teaspoon of salt evenly over the batter. Using a butter knife, swirl the salt into the batter.

3 Bake in the center of the oven for about 35 minutes, until the edges are set but the center is still a bit soft and a toothpick inserted into the center comes out coated with a little of the batter. Let cool at room temperature in the pan for 1 hour, then refrigerate just until firm, about 1 hour longer. Lift the brownie from the pan and peel off the foil. Cut into 16 squares, sprinkle with sea salt if desired and serve the brownies at room temperature.

MAKE AHEAD The brownies can be refrigerated in an airtight container for up to 3 days and frozen for up to 1 month.

Molten Chocolate Cakes *with* Peanut Butter Filling

In this fast recipe, FOOD & WINE's Grace Parisi makes molten chocolate cakes even more decadent by filling them with warm, creamy peanut butter. As a fun alternative to the peanut butter, try raspberry jam, caramel or Marshmallow Fluff.

INGREDIENTS

- 1 stick plus 1 tablespoon unsalted butter, plus melted butter for brushing
- 1 tablespoon unsweetened cocoa powder
- ¼ cup plus 1 tablespoon all-purpose flour
- 6 ounces dark chocolate (70 percent cacao), chopped
- 3 tablespoons creamy peanut butter
- 1 tablespoon confectioners' sugar, plus more for sprinkling
- ½ cup granulated sugar
- 3 large eggs, at room temperature

Pinch of salt

4 SERVINGS | ACTIVE: 15 MIN; TOTAL: 40 MIN

1 Preheat the oven to 425°. Brush four 6-ounce ramekins with melted butter. In a small bowl, whisk the cocoa powder with 1 tablespoon of the flour; dust the ramekins with the cocoa mixture, tapping out the excess. Transfer the ramekins to a sturdy baking sheet.

2 In a medium saucepan, melt 1 stick of butter with the chocolate over very low heat, stirring occasionally. Let cool slightly.

3 In a small bowl, blend the peanut butter with the 1 tablespoon of confectioners' sugar and the remaining 1 tablespoon of butter.

4 In a medium bowl, using an electric mixer, beat the granulated sugar with the eggs and salt at medium-high speed until thick and pale yellow, 3 minutes. Using a rubber spatula, fold in the melted chocolate until no streaks remain. Fold in the ¼ cup of flour.

5 Spoon two-thirds of the chocolate batter into the prepared ramekins, then spoon the peanut butter mixture on top. Cover with the remaining chocolate batter. Bake in the center of the oven for 16 minutes, until the tops are cracked but the centers are still slightly jiggly. Transfer the ramekins to a rack and let cool for 5 to 8 minutes.

6 Run the tip of a knife around each cake to loosen. Invert a small plate over each cake and, using pot holders, invert again. Carefully lift off the ramekins. Dust the warm cakes with confectioners' sugar and serve.

Milk-Chocolate-Frosted Layer Cake

While at Arrows Restaurant in Ogunquit, Maine, pastry chef Karina Gowing improved chocolate layer cake by replacing the standard buttercream frosting with an ultracreamy milk-chocolate ganache. The ganache is easy to make and spreads onto the cocoa-flavored cake more smoothly than buttercream, giving the cake a sophisticated look.

A cold glass of milk would be good with this rich cake, but a glass of nutty, toffee-scented Madeira would really complement it. Look for the Cossart Gordon 5-Year-Old Bual Madeira or the Broadbent 10-Year-Old Malmsey Madeira.

INGREDIENTS

1¼ cups cake flour

¼ cup unsweetened cocoa powder

½ teaspoon baking powder

2 sticks (8 ounces) unsalted butter

½ cup whole milk

6 large eggs, separated

1 cup sugar

Pinch of salt

1½ cups heavy cream

1½ pounds good-quality milk chocolate, finely chopped

Shaved milk chocolate, for garnish (optional)

MAKES ONE 9-INCH SQUARE LAYER CAKE
ACTIVE: 45 MIN; TOTAL: 3 HR

1 Preheat the oven to 325°. Butter and flour two 9-inch square cake pans. In a medium bowl, whisk the cake flour, cocoa and baking powder. In a medium saucepan, melt the butter in the milk over low heat. Transfer to a large bowl; let cool slightly. Whisk in the egg yolks and ½ cup of the sugar. Add the dry ingredients; whisk until smooth.

2 In a clean bowl, beat the egg whites with the salt until soft peaks form. Gradually add the remaining ½ cup sugar and beat at medium-high speed until the whites are stiff and glossy. Fold the beaten whites into the batter until no streaks remain. Divide the batter between the pans and bake for 25 minutes, until the cakes are springy and a toothpick inserted in the centers comes out clean. Transfer the cakes to a rack and let cool completely.

3 Meanwhile, in a medium saucepan, bring the cream to a simmer. Put the chopped chocolate in a heatproof bowl and pour the hot cream on top. Let stand for 3 minutes, then whisk until smooth. Let the frosting stand at room temperature, stirring occasionally, until thick enough to spread, about 1 hour.

4 Turn the cakes out of the pans and put one layer on a plate. Top with 1 cup of the frosting, spreading it to the edge. Top with the second layer and spread the remaining frosting over the top and sides. Let the cake stand at room temperature for about 30 minutes, cut into squares and garnish with chocolate shavings.

MAKE AHEAD The frosted cake can be refrigerated in an airtight container for up to 3 days.

A

B

photographers

Cedric Angeles 135

Quentin Bacon 31, 35, 43, 57, 69, 133, 141, 147, 157, 171, 185, 223, 233, 235, 239

James Baigrie 29, 47, 99, 245

Hallie Burton 25

Joseph de Leo 217

Stephanie Foley 79, 87, 103, 125, 149, 163, 169, 211

Amit Geron 15

Marie Hennechart 23

Frances Janisch 81, 191, 201, 227

John Kernick 21, 59, 67, 71, 91, 127, 155, 199, 225

Yunhee Kim 33, 63, 97

William Meppem 41

David Nicolas 85

Kana Okada 27, 51, 55, 117, 121

Con Poulos 19, 53, 61, 65, 77, 101, 107, 113, 115, 143, 151, 159, 205, 231, 241, 247

Tina Rupp 49, 75, 89, 111, 145, 161, 167, 183, 187, 189, 203, 207, 221, 229, 243

Lucy Schaeffer 13, 109, 153, 175, 193, 219

Zubin Shroff 197

Anson Smart 177, 213

Fredrika Stjärne 6, 11, 17, 37, 83, 93, 119, 123, 131, 139, 173, 179, 181, 237

Petrina Tinslay 209

Anna Williams 45, 95, 137

FOOD&WINE
BOOKS

More books from
FOOD&WINE

Annual Cookbook 2010
Over 600 recipes from the world's most sensational
cooks, including celebrity chefs like Tom Colicchio,
Rick Bayless and Bobby Flay.

Best of the Best Cookbook Recipes
The biggest names in cooking—Lidia Bastianich,
Emeril Lagasse, Thomas Keller, Patrick and Gina Neely
and others—share more than 100 tantalizing recipes.

Cocktails 2010
Cocktail and party-food recipes (more than 150 in all)
from the world's top mixologists and barchefs, plus
an indispensable guide to cocktail basics and the
world's 100 best nightspots.

Wine Guide 2010
The most up-to-date guide, with over
1,100 recommendations and an easy-to-use
tip sheet for perfect food pairings.

**Available wherever books are sold, or call 800-284-4145
or log on to foodandwine.com/books**.